T0049672

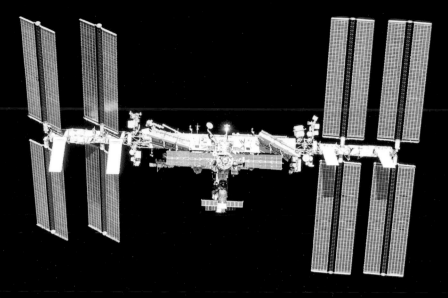

SPACE CARE

A KID'S
GUIDE TO
SURVIVING
SPACE

By Jennifer Swanson

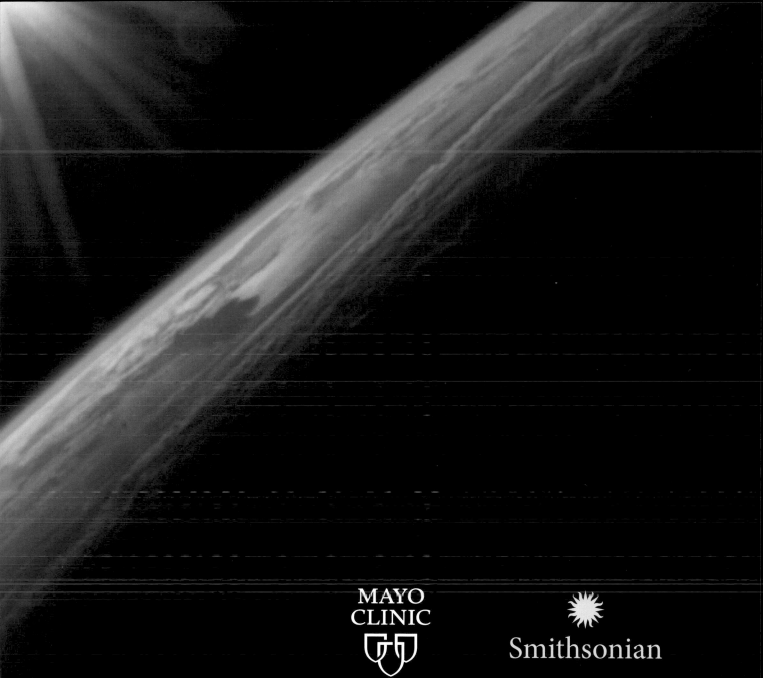

Acknowledgments
I'm very grateful to astronaut Megan McArthur for providing the awesome answers to the kids' questions. Thanks to Dr. Michael Harrison, who gave me great insight to the ways the human body behaves in microgravity. – JS

Mayo Clinic would like to thank Jan Stepanek, M.D., M.P.H., and Michael Harrison, M.D., Ph.D., aerospace medicine specialists, for their invaluable contributions to this project. The publisher would also like to thank the following at Smithsonian Enterprises: Margaret A. Weitekamp, National Air and Space Museum Curator and Department Chair, and contributing writer; Paige Towler, Editorial Lead, Licensed Publishing; Jill Corcoran, Senior Director, Licensed Publishing; Brigid Ferraro, Vice President, Business Development and Licensing; and Carol LeBlanc, President, Smithsonian Enterprises.

With special thanks to the team at NASA: Maureen O'Brien, Bert Ulrich, Gina Anderson, Daniel Huot, Chelsey Ballarte, and Megan Dean

Dedication
For my mom, Alice, a nurse, who also loved space. – JS

First edition 2023
MAYO CLINIC PRESS KIDS | An imprint of Mayo Clinic Press
200 First St. SW
Rochester, MN 55905
mcpress.mayoclinic.org
To stay informed about Mayo Clinic Press, please subscribe to our free e-newsletter at mcpress.mayoclinic.org or follow us on social media.

ISBN: 979-8-88770-007-6 (hardcover) | 979-8-88770-008-3 (ebook)
Library of Congress Control Number: 2023933324
Printed in China
CIP data available upon request.

Produced for Mayo Clinic Press Kids by WonderLab Group, LLC; Founders: Jennifer Emmett, Erica Green, Kate Hale; Picture editing by Annette Kiesow; Design by Karen Thompson; Production Design by Project Design Company

TABLE OF CONTENTS

The hazards of spaceflight are real. Imagine living for months inside a small, confined ship, crammed in with several other people. You can never open a window for fresh air and rarely get to taste fresh food. You start to lose your muscle mass and bone density. Your vision might get worse. You're exposed to high doses of radiation while traveling millions of miles from your only home and all your loved ones. And that's after you've survived the rocket ride into space. So why would anyone choose to take these risks to their mental and physical health?

We do this because we are born explorers.
(And because it's fun!)

Our curiosity drives us to push beyond the limits of what we know and what we think we can do. We gaze at the Moon, send rovers to Mars, even launch a rotorcraft to survey Titan, Saturn's largest moon! We imagine what it will be like to live there, to explore there. We are willing to endure the physical, mental, and emotional hardships in exchange for the tremendous discoveries we will make both on the journey and at the destination. Together with a team of creative problem-solvers on Earth, we work through the challenges and hazards we face to get to our destination safely.

Humans have been traveling to space for over 60 years. And for more than 20 years astronauts have lived continuously aboard the International Space Station. We conduct research in an orbit near to Earth's surface for scientists around the world, studying things like how cells change and how liquids behave in space. But astronauts are not just lab technicians; we are also test subjects. Our bodies are studied before, during, and after these long-duration missions in the weightless environment. Scientists have observed changes in our immune system, gene expression, and even how our brains control our bodies in space. Engineers and dieticians have developed special exercise equipment and diets to reduce bone loss and keep our muscles strong. Behavioral health experts consider how to use innovative technologies like virtual reality for mental health support. This work helps us find solutions to the challenges of missions to the Moon and Mars.

But this research also provides benefits for those still living on Earth. Imagine what you can do in a space lab that you cannot do on Earth! Living and working in free fall we make discoveries about biology that benefit astronaut health and support development of new vaccines for diseases back on Earth. Experiments with flames may help us design better spacecraft engines and cleaner burning car engines. We grow plants to improve astronaut diets and develop more drought-tolerant crops. We look back at our home planet for the sheer beauty of it and make observations that contribute to our understanding of Earth's changing climate.

This is exactly why we work so hard to get to space and to keep going farther. It's also why we must practice good space care for our bodies and brains while we're up there! There is always more to discover, about ourselves and about our universe.

—Megan McArthur, Astronaut

INTRODUCTION

Living in space is not like living on Earth. Space is extremely cold in the dark and very hot in direct sunlight. Gravity environments can also be different in space

On Earth, if a person throws a ball in the air or trips and falls, they know that gravity will pull the object—or them—to the ground. Gravity is a force of attraction that affects everything. While gravity still pulls on things in space, the force of gravity in space seems much smaller. So small, in fact, that it's called microgravity. In microgravity, things appear weightless. That means that heavier objects are easier to move, and people float.

Floating sounds fun! Wouldn't it be awesome to float to school? But floating instead of walking can also be a bit confusing for the brain if it can't tell which way is up or down. It can take a few days for the brain to get used to this new feeling, but astronauts don't mind. After all, they are in SPACE!

There are other changes that can affect astronauts while they are in space. One is radiation, or electromagnetic energy that is emitted from the Sun. Since the International Space Station orbits in the outer atmosphere of our planet, there is less protection from the Sun. This means astronauts are exposed to much more radiation than normal.

Of course, being in a new place, and adjusting to these changes can make it tough to sleep. Eating can be challenging, too, as the food is mostly in small packages. Astronauts even have to attach themselves to the toilet when they use the bathroom!

With all these things to deal with, how does an astronaut stay healthy while in space? It's not always easy, but they have a schedule to help them.

Astronauts work out every day to keep their muscles strong. They eat a healthy diet and have medical check-ins with their flight surgeons—the doctors assigned to monitor the astronauts on each mission.

What happens if an astronaut gets sick in space? National Aeronautics and Space Administration (NASA) doctors keep a close watch on every astronaut. As soon as astronauts feel sick, they let the doctors know. Doctors help astronauts get well again as fast as possible.

So why are humans living and working in space? The ISS is not just a place to live; it's also a laboratory. Astronauts do research to help figure out how people might one day live on the Moon or even on Mars. Read on to discover how astronauts take the best care of themselves in space.

NOT IN YOUR OWN BACKYARD

On Earth, humans typically have a place they call home. For astronauts in space, home is the International Space Station (ISS).

The ISS is temperature-controlled and does have atmospheric pressure, just like an airplane. But the one thing it doesn't have is gravity. Still, it has the most gorgeous views of our planet, which can be seen through the big cupola: spectacular lights, stars that feel close-up, and a view of the Moon fill up the dome. Living in space, however, does take some getting used to. Microgravity, radiation, and changes in temperature can leave astronauts feeling out of balance.

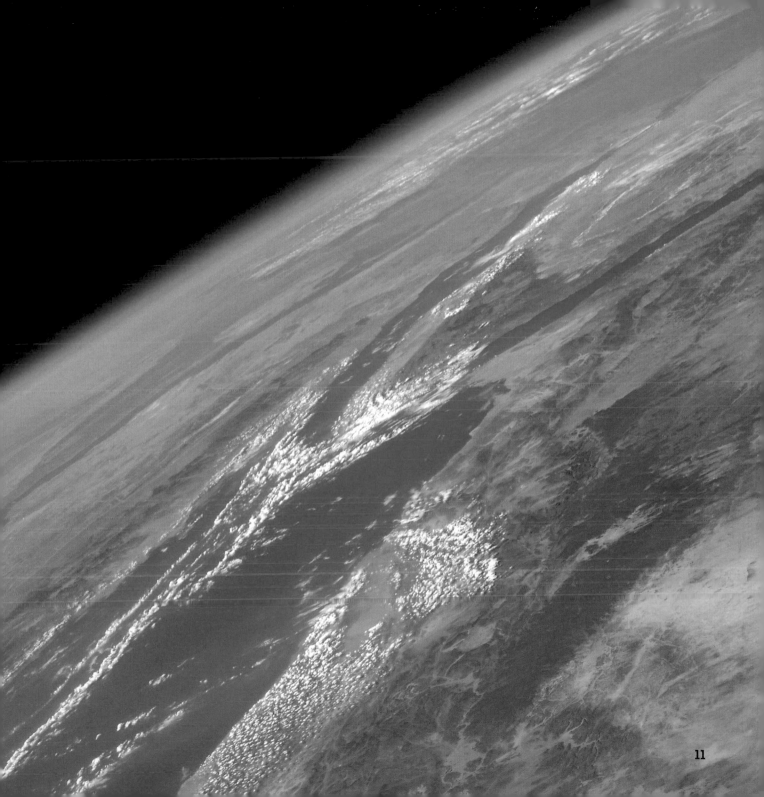

11

How Does Microgravity
AFFECT THE BODY?

Floating is fun! NASA Astronaut Jessica Watkins hangs on to a pipe while working on the ISS.

Astronauts on the ISS live in a microgravity environment. While inside—or outside—the ISS, they float. But since they are orbiting the Earth, the reason they float is a bit different. The Earth's gravity pulls objects, like the ISS toward it. So it's true to say that the ISS is constantly falling toward the Earth.

In order to stay in orbit, the ISS must maintain a constant speed of 17,500 mph, or it will get pulled into Earth's atmosphere. That speed of 17,500 mph allows the ISS to follow the curve of the Earth. So, even though the ISS is constantly falling toward Earth, if it remains on that curved path, it will never fall into the Earth's atmosphere. Just like the ISS, the objects and people inside are also in free fall, which means they float.

Although floating can be fun, living in microgravity affects the body in surprising ways. Let's start with the blood stream. Inside the human body are 60,000 miles of long tubes called blood vessels. These vessels pump blood throughout the body, from the head to the toes and back. This takes a lot of force. Your blood pressure measures the force (or pressure) on the blood as it flows through these vessels.

Blood pressure changes with position. When a person stands up, the body knows. This causes the heart to beat harder to increase the blood pressure. Higher blood pressure is needed to pump up the blood that might have pooled in the legs. When a person sits, the blood pressure adjusts again. On Earth, gravity plays a part in the force needed to move the fluid in your body. But in space, it's a different matter.

In microgravity, the body doesn't need to respond to a change in position. This is because when you're constantly floating, there is no "normal" position. Microgravity causes fluids, such as blood, to pool upward from the legs and center of the body toward the heart. And yet, it doesn't stop there.

Have you ever seen a picture of an astronaut in space? It looks like their face is full, or maybe slightly swollen. This is because the fluids in their body have shifted to their chest and head.

This extra fluid can cause headaches. It can also make an astronaut feel like they have a constant stuffy nose. They do, but it's not from a having caught a cold.

Microgravity causes the heart to change shape. Normally the heart is an oval shape (picture a water balloon), but in space the heart looks more like a round ball. No one knows exactly why this happens. It might be because the heart muscle doesn't work as hard in microgravity. Thankfully, the change is not permanent. After a few weeks back on Earth, an astronaut's heart returns to normal.

The heart isn't the only organ that's affected by microgravity. Eyes, muscles, and even a person's sense of balance can be disrupted in space. If an astronaut experiences any of these issues, they tell the NASA doctors right away. Most of these disruptions are not serious and go away after a few days. But it's always a good thing to let the doctor know just to be safe.

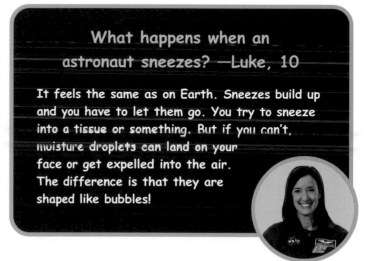

What happens when an astronaut sneezes? —Luke, 10

It feels the same as on Earth. Sneezes build up and you have to let them go. You try to sneeze into a tissue or something. But if you can't, moisture droplets can land on your face or get expelled into the air. The difference is that they are shaped like bubbles!

How Space Affects the
HUMAN BODY

The human body is conditioned to life on Earth. So when we leave our home planet, lots of weird stuff happens to us.

EYES Too much fluid in the head pushes on the optic nerve and can cause blurry vision.

SPINE Astronauts can stretch as gravity isn't pushing down on them. Muscles atrophy, or begin to waste away, due to lack of use.

BLOOD Astronauts have less blood volume in microgravity, which doesn't harm them, but is interesting.

HEART Instead of an oval, the heart is shaped more like a ball. It also pumps less fluid around in microgravity.

BRAIN Fluid in the brain increases, which can cause headaches. Extra fluid makes the astronaut's faces look round.

Eye HEALTH

Extra fluid in the head can increase the pressure on the eyes. Imagine squeezing an air-filled balloon from the bottom. The top of the balloon pushes out, stretching the material to its limit. Like the balloon, if fluid presses on the optic nerve, it will swell. The optic nerve is the "communications cable" between the brain and eyes. When the optic nerve is disturbed, vision can be affected. The back of the eye flattens out and vision may become worse, or even blurry. That's right. Astronauts that didn't need glasses on the ground, might need them in space! And if swelling happens around the optic nerve, that is not good. It can result in long-term vision problems for some astronauts.

The longer an astronaut stays in space, the greater the effect on their eyes. About one-third of astronauts that go up for less than fourteen days have some problems with their vision. If they are in space for four to six months, about two-thirds of them are affected. This problem is called Spaceflight Associated Neuro-ocular Syndrome (SANS). It's important for scientists to understand what causes SANS. Unlike the heart, the eyes don't always go back to normal when astronauts return to Earth. And if they do, it can take months. Sometimes after a visit to space, an astronaut may need to wear glasses for a while back on Earth—just until their vision returns to normal.

But how do they see while they are in space? NASA has a plan for that! Astronauts can get glasses in space—no appointment or doctor's office needed. There are glasses for seeing up close or far away; even bifocals and trifocals are available. Astronauts can also use Superfocus glasses, glasses which adjust for focus. They simply slide the button on the nose piece and change how they see!

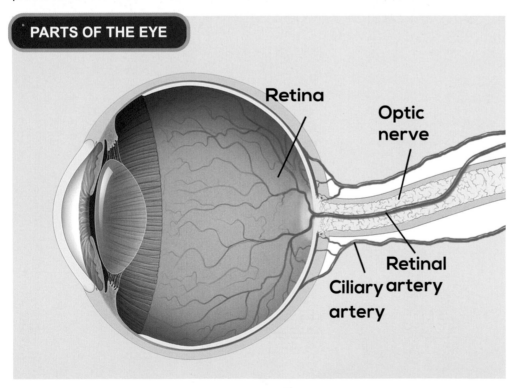

PARTS OF THE EYE

Retina

Optic nerve

Retinal artery

Ciliary artery

Eye Exams in Space!

Astronaut Karen Nyberg is giving herself an eye exam. She is using a fundoscope. This is a special instrument that looks at the retina in the back of the eye. There are also instruments that take pictures of the back of the eye. Once collected, Karen sends the data back to Earth to scientists who study vision. Doctors are hoping to figure out ways to help astronauts have healthy vision during and after spaceflight.

Eyes wide open. Astronaut Karen Nyberg uses a fundoscope to give herself an eye exam.

Can Astronauts Wear Contacts in Space?

Yes! There are many astronauts who wear contacts on the ISS. Astronauts wear gas-permeable contacts. These allow more oxygen to get to the eye (which is a good thing). They are semi-rigid, not soft. And they can be worn for up to seven days. Now all you need is a stable place to hang on to so you can put them in.

Sense of
BALANCE

All shook up. UAE Astronaut Hazzaa Ali Almansoori takes a spin in the rotating chair to see how it makes him feel.

Being weightless is cool! Imagine floating everywhere inside your house. All you would need to do is grab on to a bar and propel yourself like a ball flying through space. Awesome! And yet, that feeling can sometimes make astronauts very sick. Anyone who has ever felt motion sickness understands. Dizziness, upset stomach, drowsiness, nausea, and even vomiting are all common symptoms of motion sickness. Fast roller coasters that jerk people from side to side and send them screaming up and down big drops can cause people to get motion sickness.

But space? How can just being in space make astronauts feel sick? The human brain uses cues from both the eyes and the ears to determine balance. Eyes will show the brain that the person is upright, upside down, or sitting. On Earth, the brain understands its relationship to the ground, so it corrects for any changes. The inner ear has three tubes shaped like

How do you clean up things like vomit in space? —Gabby, 10

The best thing to do, is to be prepared! Astronauts usually get sick on their first trip to space. Everyone is given an emesis bag, or vomit bag (like the ones on planes). If you feel the urge to vomit, put the bag securely on your face and then do your business. Our bags have a nice soft cloth attached to the opening so you can wipe your face and then close the bag. You don't want to be the one who vomits into the air—then you'd have to clean it up. It would go everywhere and that's not sanitary.

loops. Each loop contains fluid and microscopic hairs. As the fluid moves, the hairs shift and send messages to the brain. They tell the brain how to stay balanced.

This system works great—on the ground. In microgravity, the brain has no idea which way is up or down. This causes problems. The result is space motion sickness, and it's not fun. Almost every astronaut experiences space motion sickness when they first arrive at the ISS. They may feel dizzy, nauseous, and very tired. Some of them even lose their appetite or vomit. It can take a couple of days for the brain to figure out what the eyes and ears are telling it. It might sound strange, but that is how humans figure out balance.

Astronauts with space motion sickness may have problems doing their work. The best way to get over space motion sickness is to take medicine. Luckily, space motion sickness generally only lasts for a short time. And the good thing is, once an astronaut has had space motion sickness, they usually don't get it again. To the brain, being in space is sort of like riding a bike—you never really forget!

Cycling in space. Astronat Sunita Williams enjoys her workout on the ISS bicycle as she keeps her muscles fit.

Keeping Muscles
STRONG

By now, the idea of floating everywhere sounds really fun, doesn't it? Not needing to walk, run, or climb stairs? Fantastic! And yet, those actions are what keep muscles strong. Not doing those activities for long periods of time weakens the muscles.

Muscles love movement. They also love resistance, a force pushing against them. On Earth, that's gravity. Space doesn't have that. And that's a problem. Without resistance, muscles can atrophy, or get thinner and weaker. Microgravity affects bones, too. Bones are

healthiest when they are used to walk, run, sit, and stand. Without gravity, bones will start to weaken from not being used. If that happens, it can cause serious issues for astronauts. After all, they are going to need those muscles when they get back to Earth or arrive on the Moon or Mars—if that is where they are headed. How can astronauts keep their muscles and bones strong in microgravity?

They work out! Astronauts spend about two-and-a-half hours a day exercising. It can be walking—or running—on a treadmill. Using the treadmill is the same in space as on Earth—except, well, astronauts can run upside down if they want. And they have to wear several tethers to keep them in place. Without the restraints, they would float away.

The Advanced Resistive Exercise Device (ARED) is another way to work out. ARED is a special weight-lifting machine. The cables on the machine act as the weights by providing resistance when pulled. Astronauts can dial up the resistance level they want, up to 150 pounds. The ARED also has a bar where astronauts can do squats, dead lifts, calf raises (for their legs), and even pull-ups. The bar provides up to 600 pounds of resistance to the user.

Eating healthy food also helps maintain healthy muscles and bones. Astronauts get meals with vitamin D, calcium, proteins, and omega-3 fatty acids to stay healthy. Doctors keep a close watch on the activity levels of the astronauts while they are in space. Even with exercise, some loss of muscle mass (the size of the muscle) and bone density (how dense the bones are) are going to happen in space.

Doctors want to be sure that no astronauts lose too much of either one before they come home. The longer a person stays in microgravity, the more it affects them. That's why sometimes you see astronauts being carried off the capsule after they return to Earth. Usually after a few months, their bone density returns to normal. Then they start working out on Earth. Regardless of where they are, astronauts need to stay in shape.

Mayo Medi-Facts

School-age kids should get about sixty minutes of exercise every day. This doesn't mean they have to actually work out. It can be walking to and from school, around school, or running during recess. The more time spent moving, the better it is for the body!

Astronaut Leland Melvin gets in his daily workout.

Do things inside us (like our blood or stomach) also float in space?
—Anil, 11

Yes—the food in your stomach floats, which can make you feel full even if you haven't eaten a lot. Your bladder also feels different when it's full. You have to learn your body's new cues for when you need to go.

Out of **SYNC**

Eye exams of the future? Astronaut Akihiko Hoshide is wearing the Drager Double Sensor on his forehead as he prepares to perform an ultrasound on his eye.

On Earth, people use the position of the Sun to know when it's time to sleep. When the Sun is up, people are awake. When the Sun goes down and it gets dark, they sleep. Unless of course someone has a job where they work at night and sleep in the day. But even then, they are still using the Sun as a guide for their sleep pattern.

That system works great if the Sun only rises and sets once in a twenty-four-hour period. But the ISS completes sixteen orbits around Earth each day. That is sixteen sunrises and sunsets. Or one every forty-five minutes! So, how do astronauts know when to sleep?

Humans have a circadian rhythm, or a sort of internal clock that helps them mark time during a twenty-four-hour period. It's a person's sleep-wake pattern. But it's usually tied to light—specifically sunlight. When an astronaut is in space, their circadian rhythm can sometimes get a little mixed up.

Their brain sees the Sun and thinks, "I should be awake." Forty-five minutes later, when a sunset occurs, their brain says, "I should be asleep." It's a never-ending pattern and one that can interfere with an astronaut's sleep.

To combat insomnia, the LED lights in the ISS are changed throughout the day. Blue light, or the light you get from a computer, keeps people awake. This is why blue lights are used during daylight hours on the ISS. It makes the brain think it's time to be up and working.

As the day goes on, the lights on the ISS shift to emit less blue light. This change signals the astronaut's circadian rhythm that it is becoming later in the day. Hopefully, this helps the astronaut's brain understand that night is near.

But it's still tough to sleep in space. Sometimes astronauts have to work really long hours or at night.

They might be excited for an event—like an upcoming spacewalk—and not be able to sleep. (This happens here on Earth, too!) Also, it is quite noisy on the ISS from all of the machines running constantly. Earplugs can help, but not always.

When an astronaut finds it hard to sleep, they talk to the NASA doctors to get tips. First, they might try relaxation techniques, like meditation or deep breathing. An astronaut can adjust the temperature of their sleeping area. Maybe they are too cold or too hot. All of these things can cause a person not to sleep (even on Earth).

If none of that works, doctors may prescribe medication. Many astronauts take medication while in space to help them sleep. They won't need the medication to sleep when they are back home.

Sleeping is important. An astronaut can't perform their job well if they are tired. How easy do you think going on a six-hour spacewalk is without sleep? It's not easy, and it could be dangerous. That's why doctors are very aware of every astronaut's sleep schedule. The goal is for each astronaut to get at least six hours of sleep every twenty-four-hour period.

Mayo Medi-Facts

Insomnia is the inability to fall asleep. Insomnia can also happen if you fall asleep, wake up, and then can't get back to sleep. It's a common problem. And an annoying one, too. Everyone feels much better when they get enough sleep. Lack of sleep can leave a person cranky, tired, and out of sorts. If you are having insomnia, talk to your parents and your doctor. They will have suggestions for how to get to sleep!

ZZZZZ ...

Rad REACTIONS

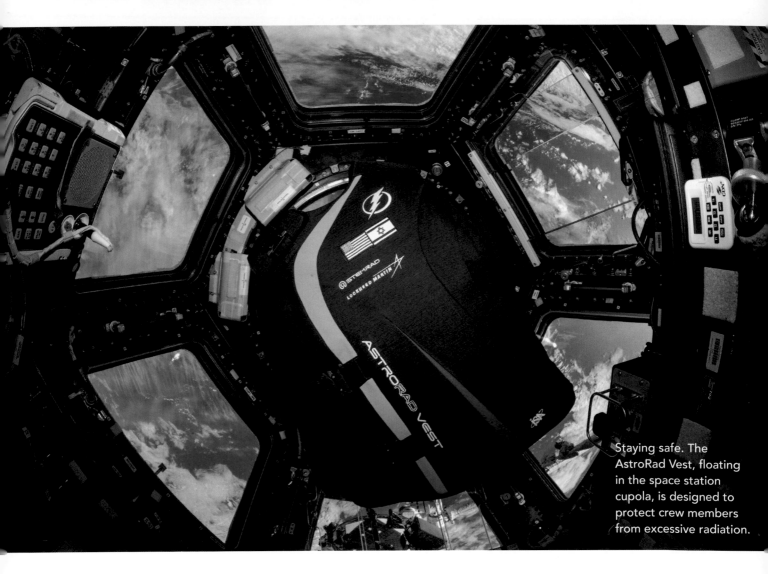

Staying safe. The AstroRad Vest, floating in the space station cupola, is designed to protect crew members from excessive radiation.

Microgravity is not the only thing that can mess with an astronaut's body. Radiation in space can do it, too. What is radiation? Radiation is an invisible energy that moves throughout space as waves and particles. The biggest source of radiation is the Sun. But radiation can come from microwaves lights, X-rays, and more. In space, radiation can also come from cosmic rays, solar flares (explosions on the Sun), and from Earth's magnetic field.

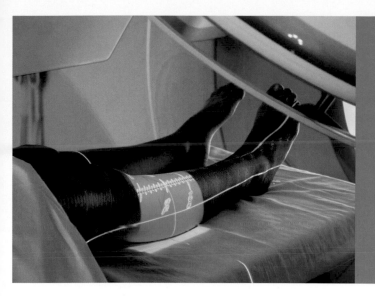

Mayo Medi-Facts

If radiation is so harmful to the body, why is it used to treat cancer? Just like normal cells, cancer cells are destroyed by radiation. Targeting cancer cells with beams of high-energy radiation can cause them to die off. While this process does destroy healthy cells, it hopefully destroys the cancer cells first.

Earth's atmosphere shields humans from most of the intense radiation from sunlight. The ISS, located two hundred miles above Earth's surface, does not have that same protection. The inhabitants of the ISS get exposed to higher doses of harmful radiation. Radiation exposure is cumulative. This means the longer a person is exposed, the higher the dose.

What does radiation do to the human body? Radiation can change cells. It breaks down DNA, the genetic material that tells cells how to grow and divide. Loss of cells can damage organs, making them not work as well. Radiation can also cause cancers to grow. Excessive radiation can damage the central nervous system. This could cause problems with behavior or motor (movement) functions. If the damage is severe enough, a person can develop acute radiation syndrome (ARS).

It is important for astronauts to monitor their radiation exposure. While inside the ISS, they are getting higher doses of radiation than when they are on Earth. When they go on a spacewalk, they are exposed to even more radiation. This is why the ISS has been equipped with dosimeters.

A dosimeter measures the amount of radiation in an area. It gives a reading in units of millisieverts (mSv). Every person receives about 3 mSv a year just from living on Earth. Astronauts who stay on the ISS for six months or more can receive between 50 and 120 mSv of radiation. That's almost the equivalent of twenty to four hundred years of normal background radiation on Earth. While it seems like a lot, it's not life-threatening.

Still, NASA has set a limit for the total amount of radiation an astronaut can be exposed to at 600 mSv. That's over their entire career, not all at once.

Research is still being done on this important topic. NASA needs to understand the dangers of long-term radiation exposure. The future inhabitants of the Moon (and Mars) will depend on this information to stay healthy.

The ISS is like living in a six-bedroom house with your best friends. Even though it's pretty fun, you get very little time to yourself. It can be tough to sleep. And you can't go outside for a walk—well, not without asking first. So, what's it really like to live in space?

While not all of the astronauts on the ISS may know each other before they arrive, being in a space about the size of an American football field with only two bathrooms helps people get to know each other quickly. There are places to sleep, places to work, and a place to eat. The ISS even has its own garden (although unlike gardens on Earth, this one doesn't have soil).

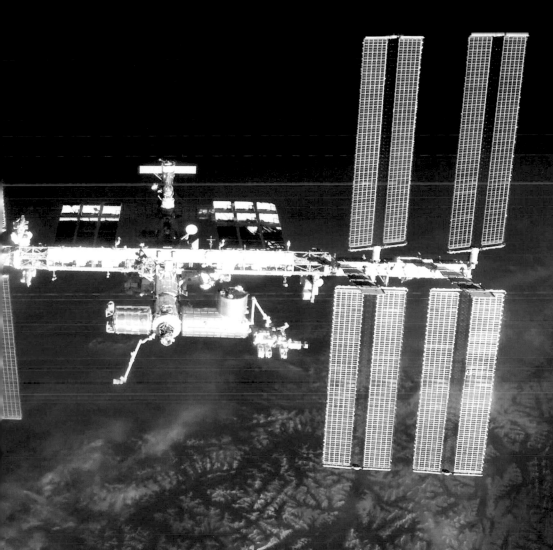

27

PIZZA **PARTY**

Living in space takes adjustment. Astronauts are without their families, friends, and pets. They live in small spaces with other people they may have just met. And they might have a hard time sleeping. It sounds like the first sleepover at a new friend's house. Everything is different.

But then the new friend pulls out your favorite food and things start to look better. There's a reason people use the term "comfort food." Food reminds people of places, friends, and family, and it brings new friends together. It's more than just eating; food can provide community.

It's a good thing that astronauts have a lot of food to choose from. The majority of their food comes in vacuumed-sealed packages. This keeps the food contained as it is eaten and cuts down on crumbs, which do not fall to the ground like they do on Earth. Crumbs fly around the ISS and get stuck in control panels and can cause problems. This is why they don't eat bread up there—too many crumbs! Instead, astronauts use tortillas.

Astronauts can choose from chicken, beef, macaroni and cheese, fruits, nuts, seafood, candy, brownies, and much more. Still, sometimes they long for comfort food from home. Astronauts can request their favorite snacks to be packed on resupply missions, including candy. Astronaut Tim Peake had his favorite bacon sandwich sent up.

Astronauts get creative with the supplies they have. Astronaut Terry Virts created a "space cheeseburger" (on a tortilla). And in 2017, NASA sent up a special pizza kit. The astronauts threw their own pizza party on the ISS. They made pizzas the regular way: They spread sauce on thin crusts and added cheese and many toppings, like olives, pepperoni, and more. Then they cooked the pizzas in the induction oven. Who doesn't like a pizza party?

The cool thing is that astronauts play with their food. Seriously! They even make videos of themselves doing it. They squeeze an entire pouch of pudding onto a spoon and then float over it and take a bite. They have to tape their tortillas to the table to spread peanut butter and jelly on them. And they even make "flying" space pizzas! These are real pizzas the astronauts make from scratch. They simply give their pizzas a push to test their ability to float before putting them into the space oven. Wouldn't it be nice if Earth parents let their kids play with their food like that?

All play aside, eating is mostly done for nutrition. Astronauts eat three meals a day: breakfast, lunch, and dinner. They can choose what they want to eat, but they do have daily calorie counts to keep.

Drinks are available, too. Tea, coffee, orange juice, lemonade, and fruit punch are always around on the ISS—straws required! Not exactly how many people are used to drinking their morning coffee.

While NASA tries to provide a variety of food and drink, astronauts who live on the ISS for a long period of time can get a little bored with it. As astronaut Don Thomas once said, "No one goes to space for the food … but the views are amazing."

Mayo Medi-Facts

It's a good thing that the ISS is supplied with fresh fruits and vegetables. These are foods that help support a healthy brain and body. To be your healthiest, try the 1-2-3 method. Eat one serving of fruits or veggies at breakfast, two at lunch, and three at dinner.

What happens if food gets stuck in your throat in space? — Moshe, 13

If food gets stuck in an astronaut's throat in space, they can clear their throat just like on Earth. But if they're really choking, then the Heimlich maneuver is needed. It would be a little different in space because the person doing it would have to hook their feet somewhere to get leverage, but it would still save someone from choking!

What's Spicy IN SPACE?

Playing with your food? Expedition 42 commander, astronaut Barry "Butch" Wilmore, shows off his juggling talents with a few mustard bottles.

The food on the ISS is pretty good. But many astronauts agree that it could use more spice. Astronaut Peggy Whitson wrote in her journal that "It's all about the sauce." She once even jokingly threatened to not let the new astronauts in when they docked at the ISS unless they had brought new sauces. Spice is serious stuff on the ISS!

Even astronauts that don't eat spicy stuff on Earth are seen dousing their food with hot sauce or chili sauce. What's the deal? Adding spice to food is more than just a preference. Remember, in space, the body fluids push up into the head. This causes stuffiness in the nose. It's like having a cold. On Earth, people with colds have a hard time tasting food. It makes sense that astronauts in space might have the same problem.

The solution? Add some spice! Sauces on board include hot sauce, wasabi, horseradish, and salsa. The standard ketchup and mustard are always available—as are salt and pepper, but not in their normal form. In space, astronauts use liquid salt and pepper! Strange, isn't it? It's important that tiny particles of salt and pepper aren't flying around the ISS.

The best thing is that the food is as international as the crew. Sushi, a Japanese specialty, is a hit with astronauts on the ISS. As is Russian tvorog (a tangy cottage cheese made sweet with fruit and nuts). There's also borscht, a Russian soup. Astronauts continue to experiment with the space food menu. Who knows what they will come up with next?

TECHNO

TREATMENTS

Some of the oldest technology on the ISS is used every day: Velcro, or that tape-like product that allows things to stick together. Apollo astronauts were using Velcro to attach equipment to the walls back in the 1960s. The objects could be attached easily and removed quickly with a fast *rrrriiippp* off the wall. Every food packet that is shipped to the ISS has a Velcro attachment. This makes it easy to keep food from floating away.

Space Peppers

No need to wait for supplies, astronauts are now growing chili peppers in space! The forty-eight seeds were flown up on a resupply mission. On the ISS, they use clay instead of dirt to grow things. Astronaut Shane Kimbrough added a special time-release fertilizer to the seed "carrier," or container, and waited. They hoped they'd have chili peppers in about four months. It worked! The peppers grew and were very tasty. Now astronauts don't have to wait for the next resupply mission to spice up their food.

Toilet TIME

Time to go! A view taken of the ISS Universal Waste Management System, (the toilet the astronauts use).

How do you go to the bathroom in space? This is a question astronauts get all the time. It makes sense. Going to the bathroom is a normal, natural part of life. The need to go to the bathroom is the same in space as on Earth. An astronaut's body tells them when it's time to go. But how do they actually do that? The answer might be surprising. After all, microgravity makes peeing, well, interesting.

The first thing to know is that the bathroom is not called a bathroom. NASA calls it a waste and hygiene compartment, or WHC. The WHC looks similar to a Porta Potty that you might find on Earth. But what's inside is very different.

This is one of two toilets on the ISS. It looks a bit daunting, doesn't it? What is the hose for? And why is there a control panel in there?

TREATMENTS

Water is precious on the ISS. It is pulled from every place possible, even urine. About 93 percent of the water-based liquids are recycled in the water recovery system. Fluids from the toilet, sweat, making coffee, or astronauts washing up are used by the water recovery system. The barrel-size tank (which is part of the water recovery system) distills the water and sanitizes it for drinking. (Don't try that at home.)

Let's take it step by step. There is a small seat.

Under the seat is a container that holds the waste. The long hose with a funnel-shaped cup on the end is where the urine goes. The primary control panel on the wall controls the urine processor assembly (UPA). When three of the yellow lights form a V shape, the astronaut can go.

The valve near the end of the hose operates the entire UPA system. Just turn it, and the vacuum fan is activated. Wait. Why would you need a vacuum for a toilet? On Earth, urine automatically falls down into the toilet because of gravity. But in microgravity, liquids float. Floating urine? Ew. The vacuum is needed to suck the urine into the hose. The hose needs to be fairly close to the body to ensure the urine goes where it should.

Once the astronaut is done urinating, they turn the valve on the hose again. The suction stops. Then, they use a disinfectant wipe to clean out the funnel. All ready for the next person.

Going number two, or poop, is a little more complicated. First, an astronaut sits on the toilet. They may place their feet onto the supports provided or use the handholds on the wall. This keeps them attached to the toilet while they are going.

They get settled over the small hole in the seat. It's only five or six inches across, so not very big. Under the hole in the seat is a plastic liner in the container. That is where the poop goes.

Once they are done with their business. They use a wipe, just like toilet paper, and place that into the plastic bag, too. The bag is folded over and pushed down into the container underneath the toilet. (There's a special stick for that, so they don't have to use their hands.) Then it's time to put on a new plastic bag for the next person. Bet gravity is sounding very good right now, isn't it?

The container beneath the toilet can hold about thirty uses. The full container is transferred to the resupply container where it will burn up as it enters Earth's atmosphere.

What's That Smell?

Living in very close quarters with others can be interesting. When people sweat, they have a scent. And well, sometimes the WHC might get fragrant. How can smells be eliminated if the windows can't be opened?

The ISS is equipped with two micropurification units. They pull tiny particulates out of the air and keep everything smelling clean and fresh. With daily exercise required for all astronauts, the ISS can smell a little like a locker room.

Hanging
AROUND

Sleeping in space is not quite like a big slumber party. But it could be close. Everyone sleeps in sleeping bags. And there are people up at all hours of the night. There is one big difference. The sleeping bags astronauts use are not spread out on the floor.

It's not possible to tell which way is up and which way is down on the ISS. So, it really doesn't matter how the sleeping bags are arranged. Astronauts can sleep hanging against the wall, secure in their own little crew cabins. Or they can sleep on the equivalent of a hammock strung between two walls.

Wherever they can get comfortable and fall asleep is best. Assuming they are out of the way of the other astronauts who might be working at night. The sleeping bags have zippers to make it easy for astronauts to get into them. They can zip their arms inside (so they don't float up). Or they can keep their arms out and let them free float.

Since astronauts don't have beds, they don't feel like they are laying down. They say it feels like standing up. Or just floating around. It's not an uncomfortable feeling, just a strange one. Until they get used to it, that is.

Time for some Zzzzs … NASA astronaut Kjell Lindgren is all zipped up for a nap in his crew sleeping bag.

Sleeping to the Moon

The Orion spacecraft, the capsule that will take astronauts to the Moon, has newly designed sleeping bags. Each astronaut will have their own bag slung across the capsule. They can use their tablets or read books by putting their arms through armholes. And every one of the six windows will have blackout shades.

The crew cabins are small yet comfortable. Each cabin only fits one person. Astronaut Sunita Williams said that "it's sort of like a little phone booth." Astronauts climb into them and then get into their sleeping bags. The weird thing is that astronauts don't feel the weight of a blanket. And it's not easy to snuggle up with a pillow under your head. Microgravity prevents all of that. Astronauts have to resort to interesting fixes to get comfortable sometimes. Kelly said he basically stuck Velcro on his head to keep his pillow in place.

The biggest danger is having enough airflow while sleeping. Like all humans, astronauts exhale carbon dioxide when they sleep. In microgravity, the carbon dioxide can form a bubble around their heads. That could cause them to suffocate. The bubble would force them to breathe in carbon dioxide, not oxygen. So that's why the crew cabins have air vents. The astronauts sleep near air vents to keep the air moving across them, which prevents the carbon dioxide bubbles from forming.

Regardless of where they sleep, the goal is that the astronauts do get to sleep. That's not always easy. While they are given eight-and-a-half hours every day in their schedule to sleep, many only get about six hours. Still, rest and relaxation are always a good idea. Sometimes just looking out the window at the amazing views is a great way to rest.

Movie
NIGHT

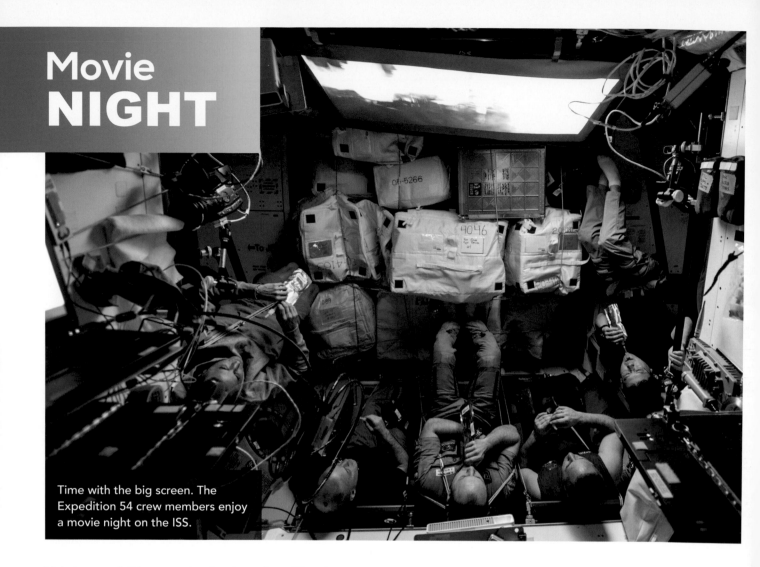

Time with the big screen. The Expedition 54 crew members enjoy a movie night on the ISS.

This leaves 5.5 hours a day for downtime. That is, unless an astronaut has to work "overtime" to prepare for a spacewalk, a new crew coming aboard, or check on experiments.

Every week each astronaut gets one-and-a-half days off. It's not quite a two-day weekend, but it's close. Unfortunately, they can't take a hike in the woods or head to the beach.

So, what do astronauts do with their time off? It's pretty similar to what people do on Earth. They play video games, call their loved ones, and read. Astronauts might also find time to hang out in the cupola, which is a cool round area of the ISS with a lot of windows. The cupola has the best views of space! Earth looks particularly amazing from low earth orbit, where the ISS is located.

Some astronauts use their cameras to take amazing pictures through the cupola's windows.

Astronauts can play music or perhaps get a few friends together to play a game of cards. Maybe they will write in their journal or read a book. A few astronauts even started a program called Story Time From Space, where they videotape themselves reading picture books aloud in space. It's pretty popular with Earth kids.

The best nights are movie nights! That's when all of the astronauts come together to watch a movie. Just like on Earth, they might make special food, like pizza. While they can't have popcorn, there are plenty of other snacks available. They turn on their high-definition projector and pull down the sixty-five-inch screen. Sometimes they rig up bungee cord seats to make themselves comfortable.

What do they watch? They've seen *Star Wars* movies, *Die Hard*, *Alien*, and many more. There are more than five hundred DVDs for them to choose from. And if their favorite movie isn't there? An astronaut can request that it be sent up on the next resupply mission.

Many astronauts take time on the weekends to have a video call with their families. They can call Earth on their own laptops. The chat can take place in their crew quarters or even in the cupola. Sometimes astronauts will go into the JEM (Japanese Experiment Module) to do somersaults for their families. Staying in touch with loved ones is definitely encouraged.

Astronauts work long hours. Their daily schedule is pretty packed. They have:

- 8.5 hours of sleep
- 6.5 hours of work
- 2.5 hours for exercise
- 3 hours for eating, getting ready, chores
- 1-2 hours for planning conferences

Mayo Medi-Facts

Some great tips for getting a good night's sleep from the Mayo Clinic:

- **Stick to a schedule—go to bed at the same time every night.**

- **Create a restful environment— turn off cell phones and any digital or video displays. These can distract you and keep you awake.**

- **Try deep breathing— If you can't get to sleep because your brain is racing, try breathing deeply. Think about something fun and relaxing. Allow your body to relax while breathing deep. Eventually, your brain will succumb to sleep.**

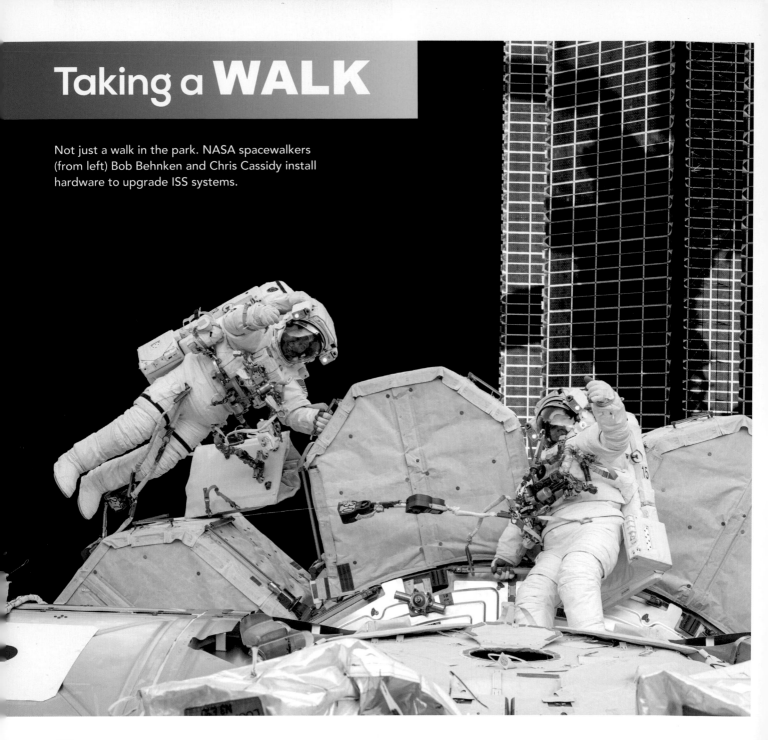

Taking a WALK

Not just a walk in the park. NASA spacewalkers (from left) Bob Behnken and Chris Cassidy install hardware to upgrade ISS systems.

Going outside is easy on Earth. Just open the door and go. Going outside of the ISS, however, is a bit more complicated.

Spacewalks are planned months or even years in advance. And they have a special name: extravehicular activity (EVA). Of course, spacewalks require lots of preparation.

First of all, the astronaut must don a spacesuit. It's more than just a suit, however. A spacesuit has its own life support system. Think of it as a personal spacecraft just for the astronaut. Why do they need all that stuff? The vacuum of space has huge swings in temperature. In the darkness or shade of space, it is extremely cold. When the Sun is shining in space, it's really hot. Plus, there's no oxygen. A spacesuit provides an astronaut with oxygen, a comfortable temperature, and the right amount of pressure. If an astronaut was exposed to space without a spacesuit, they'd die in minutes.

All of the air would be sucked out of the astronaut's lungs very quickly. The fluids within their body would boil. And their face, particularly their nose and mouth, would freeze. See why it's important that astronauts wear spacesuits?

Given all the potential dangers astronauts face, it's important that they find a spacesuit that fits. That might sound easy, but it's not. There is no closet with multiple sizes of spacesuits on the ISS. A few sizes of spacesuit components are made, and the astronauts have to fit into them. The spacesuit should be snug, but not tight. It should allow freedom of movement but also be secure and completely sealed from the outside.

Now the astronaut can start preparing to go on their spacewalk. Easy, right? Just put on the suit and head outside. Not quite. Before an astronaut can go on a spacewalk, they must follow a process that can take several hours.

It can take up to an hour to put on a spacesuit. It takes time to ensure everything is secured properly. The suit is pressurized, so everything must be sealed. Once inside

the suit, the astronaut starts breathing pure oxygen. Breathing pure oxygen removes the nitrogen gas that is normally in their blood from their body. Why is this important?

There is no atmospheric pressure in space. This means that gases can form easily in the body and tissues. If the astronaut had nitrogen in their blood, it could turn into bubbles. It's like when divers go deep in the ocean and get the bends. Astronauts can also get the bends.

After the astronaut has breathed pure oxygen for a couple of hours to remove the extra nitrogen from their body, they are ready. The astronaut puts on their safety tether, which is a rope that keeps them attached to the ISS. Then they slip on their SAFER, Simplified Aid For EVA Rescue. This backpack contains small jet thrusters to help the astronaut fly around. It's a safety feature in case they become untethered.

After exiting through the airlock—a special set of double doors that keeps the spaceship airtight—out they go. Spacewalks last from six to eight hours. They are well planned and keep the astronaut busy. When it's time to go in, the astronaut returns to the airlock, enters it, and begins to take off their suit once the airlock has been safely pressurized. Whew! That is a lot to do for just a walk outside.

Out for A WALK

A spacewalk, or extravehicular activity (EVA) occurs when the astronauts step out into space from the ISS. They are, of course, wearing a spacesuit, also known as an EMU, or EXTRAVEHICULAR MOBILITY UNIT. The spacesuit keeps them at the right temperature, pressure, and provides oxygen. Spacewalks allow astronauts to make repairs to the ISS, conduct science experiments, or just take in the beauty of the Earth from a completely unique view.

In October 2019, the first ever spacewalk with two women astronauts took place. Astronauts Jessica Meir and Christina Koch stepped outside to repair part of the solar array. This spacewalk was postponed from March 2019, when it was discovered that there weren't two spacesuits that would fit both women safely. Astronauts wearing a spacesuit that doesn't fit properly won't be able to move easily. Their visibility might also be affected. It's better to be safe than encounter problems on the spacewalk.

NASA astronauts Jessica Meir (left) and Christina Koch (right)

With the Earth 250 miles below, NASA astronaut Jessica Meir is pictured tethered to the outside of the International Space Station during a seven-hour, 17-minute spacewalk.

Aerospace Medicine Artifacts

Most people know the Smithsonian as the world's largest museum complex. They visit the 21 museums and the National Zoo to learn about history, art, culture, and science through exhibits. But did you know that is just one part of what museums do? The Smithsonian's museums are also like libraries, but with things (artifacts) instead of books. Each museum holds carefully selected (curated) objects that will tell stories of art, history, culture, or science for generations to come. The Smithsonian's National Air and Space Museum has the special duty of collecting artifacts about the history of aviation and space exploration. And that includes the history of aerospace medicine.

Years before any person launched into space, researchers worked to learn everything they could about how the forces of flight would affect the body. One remarkable artifact from that history is the Sonic Wind 1 rocket sled. Imagine strapping yourself into a red metal jet pilot's seat on top of a long black

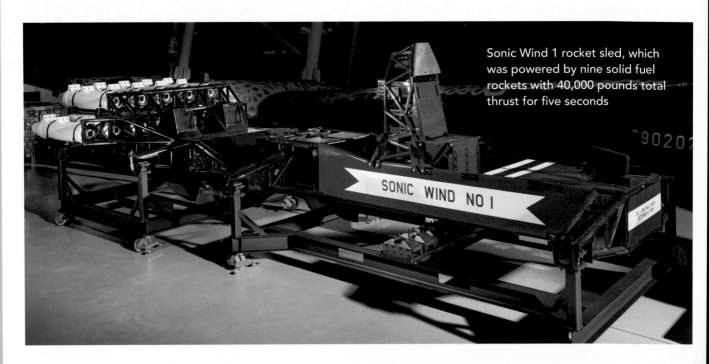

Sonic Wind 1 rocket sled, which was powered by nine solid fuel rockets with 40,000 pounds total thrust for five seconds

structure like a small flatbed train car. But on the back end, there are nine solid fuel rockets! That's what U.S. Air Force researcher Dr. John Paul Stapp did 29 different times. When those rockets fired, they produced 40,000 pounds total thrust for five seconds, hurling the sled down a track. A system of water dams at the end of the track then stopped the sled quickly. When it did, Dr. Stapp experienced as much as 22 times the force of gravity (22 g's). That's some jolt!

Stapp was not the only test subject, but he was a frequent one. The experiments were trying to learn about how the human body experiences speeding up (acceleration) and slowing down (deceleration), especially when big changes happen quickly. On December 10, 1954, during Stapp's last ride on the rocket sled, it—and he—went up to 632 miles per hour. He experienced more than 40 g's, the highest G-force any human had endured to that time. Dr. Stapp became known as "the fastest man on Earth."

The research done with the Sonic Wind 1 rocket sled showed how pilots would feel in airplanes. But it also taught scientists about acceleration and deceleration in cars. And during rocket launches and spacecraft landings. The field became known as aerospace medicine because its findings covered both aviation and spaceflight. Aerospace medicine is very important; airplanes and spacecraft can be engineered differently, but the person inside cannot.

NASA astronaut John H. Glenn, Jr., was actually an aerospace medicine test subject during his famous flight in February 1962 as the first American to orbit the Earth. That was not his main job. But in addition to making the spaceflight, he was also reporting on how being in space affected his body. That included his eyesight. Glenn's *Friendship 7* Mercury spacecraft is now part of the National Air and Space Museum's collection. The interior has been preserved, including the pieces of paper attached to the console: typed checklists, color coding for switches, and two small paper eye charts. During his three orbits, Glenn used the charts to test whether being in space affected his sight.

These are just some of the many artifacts that the museum holds. There is also space food, including some pieces flown—but not eaten—during Apollo 11, the first human landing on the Moon. Other artifacts include samples of technologies used to allow astronauts to go to the bathroom, to sleep in space, and to keep themselves clean and healthy.

Going forward, lots of different kinds of people—and more diverse body types—will be participating in spaceflight.

And the museum will keep collecting.

Mercury Capsule, MA-6, *Friendship 7*

Spacesuits

Part of being healthy and at home in space is the ability to go outside the spacecraft or space station to do repairs, upgrades, or maintenance. That requires a spacesuit. Spacesuits might seem like regular clothing. But spacesuits are really human-sized (and -shaped) spaceships, which is especially true when

they're used for spacewalks. At the Smithsonian's National Air and Space Museum, spacesuits are also important artifacts. They show the history of how people learned to protect astronauts from the dangers of space.

Consider Alan Shepard's Mercury spacesuit. He wore the close-fitting silver spacesuit when he became the first American in space during a suborbital flight in May 1961. The Mercury spacesuit was a two-layer, full-pressure suit. The B.F. Goodrich Company designed it. They based it on their Mark IV pressure suit used by Naval aviators. Instead of working inside a cockpit, it protected Shepard inside the spacecraft. No spacewalking in this early suit!

The museum also has Neil Armstrong's A7-L Apollo 11 spacesuit, the very one he wore when he was the first human to step onto the Moon in July 1969. It was designed especially for walking on the lunar surface. Twenty-one different layers protected the moonwalker. There is still lunar dust on it. Displaying it requires a special case to control temperature, lighting, moisture, and airflow.

Spacesuits do not need to have flown in space to be important. Prototypes or early models are also significant. They show how spacesuits were developed. Before creating the final suits, engineers create prototypes to test different pieces (components). For example, the museum has the AX-1L developmental suit created by the International Latex Company (ILC) in the 1960s. ILC engineers used it to try to get the contract to build suits designed for moonwalks. (Spoiler: They won!) The AX-1L included rubberized joints much like the ones later used in the real lunar spacesuits. But the

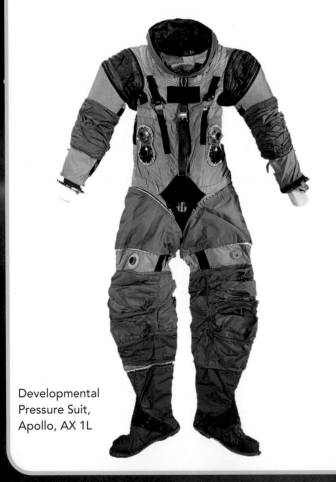

Developmental Pressure Suit, Apollo, AX 1L

suit's front zipper bent too much when worn. And overall, the AX-1L was just not comfortable. The engineers used what they learned in the next designs (including putting the zipper in the back).

Spacesuits used to be custom measured especially for each astronaut. The orange spacesuits worn for launches and landings aboard the space shuttle orbiters were not custom made, but they were adjusted for each person. Because of their bright color—which would be seen easily in an emergency—the astronauts called them "pumpkin suits." There were actually two different kinds of pumpkin suits: the Launch Entry Spacesuits (LES) worn between 1988 and 1994 and the Advanced Crew Escape Suit (ACES) used between 1994 and 2011, when space shuttle orbiters stopped flying. A new version of the ACES is being planned for the astronauts returning to the Moon aboard the Orion spacecraft.

Now the spacesuits used for spacewalks have parts that fit together to match the astronaut's size, like separates.

Pick a top (hard upper torso or HUT) and pair it with a bottom. And then start practicing! When preparing for a spacewalking mission, astronauts spend a long time rehearsing the planned tasks. They are also getting used to the spacesuits.

Whatever their uses, spacesuits are challenging artifacts to keep in good condition for a long time. To build the best ones, engineers often experiment with new metals, coatings, and fabrics. They want materials that are either flexible, or rigid, or puncture-resistant, or durable, as needed. That means that the museum's conservators (scientists who figure out how to preserve artifacts) have to care for lots of different materials.

Who knows? Maybe someday, the museum's conservators will be working on a spacesuit that you designed! Or will it be one that you wore?

The Launch-Entry Suit (LES) was a partial-pressure suit worn by Space Shuttle crew members for protection against loss of cabin pressure during the critical ascent and descent phases of a mission.

—Margaret A. Weitekamp,
Curator and Department Chair, Space History Department,
National Air and Space Museum, Smithsonian

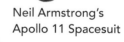

Neil Armstrong's Apollo 11 Spacesuit

CHAPTER THREE

IS THERE A DOCTOR IN THE HOUSE?

Living in space is awesome, but, just like on Earth, things happen. People get sick, have accidents, and even feel a little lonely. How do astronauts handle all these things? Constant checkups and doctors that are just a video call away definitely help.

What a view! Astronaut Peggy Whitson pauses during a busy day on orbit to look out the seven-windowed cupola at the Earth 250 miles below. The cupola module, which affords a glorious view of Earth with its seven windows is common place for astronauts to spend downtime.

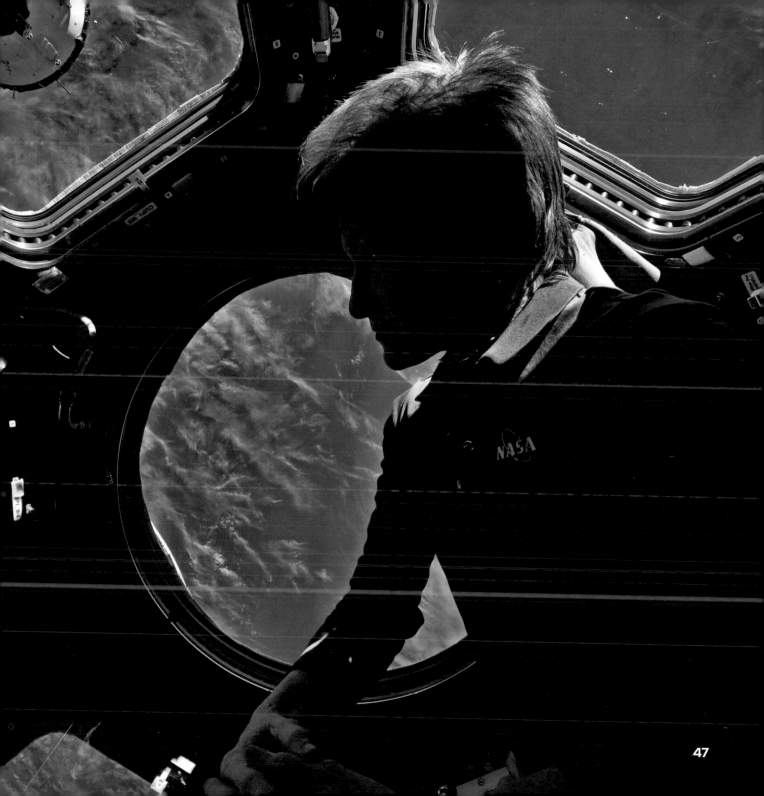

CHECKUP!

Time for a checkup! NASA astronaut and medical doctor, Serena Auñón-Chancellor draws (ESA) astronaut Alexander Gerst's blood.

Just like on Earth, astronauts get medical checkups. The ones in space, though, happen much more often. Doctors schedule weekly talks with each astronaut. But in between, astronauts are supposed to evaluate themselves. They should report anything that seems odd about their health. Do they feel dizzy? Nauseous? Overly tired? These might be symptoms of space motion sickness.

If they are having problems sleeping or eating, they need to let the flight surgeon know. And if they have any pain or other issues that are bothering them, it's time to tell the doctor.

But astronauts also perform tests on themselves or others to keep informed about their health. And many of these procedures are also done for research. That's right. The astronauts are providing data to scientists on the ground about how humans are affected by microgravity.

One of the big things astronauts do is take their own blood. While this might seem like something you'd never do, it's really not that difficult.

Sound easy? It's probably not something everyone would be willing to do. Before they go up into space, astronauts learn how to draw their own blood. Collecting their blood allows scientists to learn so much about how the human body reacts to microgravity. This is so important for future long-term missions to the Moon or even Mars.

Astronauts don't have to take their blood every day, but they may have to do it a couple of times while in space. Aside from taking blood, they check their blood pressure, check their eyes, and even take ultrasounds of their bodies, just for research.

Individual Checkups

Astronauts perform checkups on themselves and report their findings to the flight surgeon. They check their blood pressure and temperature. They do many checks on their eyes since eyesight can change drastically in space. And they even check their ears.

NASA astronaut (and medical doctor) Andrew Morgan participates in a hearing test to help doctors understand how the microgravity environment and the acoustic levels of the station affect a crewmember's hearing before, during, and after a mission.

Astronaut Akihiko Hoshide undergoing a generic blood draw.

Sick DAYS

The first time a new spacecraft is opened, astronauts wear masks to keep safe from unwanted particles that might have come up on the spacecraft.

People on Earth get to stay home if they are sick. An astronaut that feels sick can also take a day off, although it rarely happens. If they don't feel well enough, they can have a day where they do light duty. Or perhaps take some of the day off. But usually, that doesn't happen too often. Other than space sickness, which is quite common, most astronauts stay fit throughout their mission.

Keeping astronauts healthy starts a long time before the launch. In order to qualify to become an astronaut, a person must pass the long-duration astronaut

A stuffed-up nose from filled sinuses can last for days. In microgravity, unfortunately, the sinuses don't drain well. Also, NASA has learned that germs seem to thrive in microgravity. This means that sometimes sinus infections can set in. If that happens, astronauts can take medicine to help, but most likely they just have to wait it out.

Astronauts are constantly monitored by the NASA flight surgeon on the ground. The flight surgeon meets with each astronaut individually. They chat on a video call. The conversation is private, as it's covered under medical privilege. But the astronaut can feel free to tell the doctor anything they might tell a doctor on Earth. It's like being in a doctor's office. Well, with a better view.

physical (LDAP). The LDAP is an assessment of a person's physical and mental abilities. It also includes a comprehensive medical checkup. They must have good eyesight, coordination, a strong respiratory system, and be in excellent health. NASA wants to ensure that each potential astronaut has no medical issues that could cause a problem while in space.

Once an astronaut is chosen to go to space, NASA takes every precaution to be sure that they are healthy. Two weeks before the launch, astronauts are placed into quarantine. They are given medical exams, which might include swabbing their noses to check for viruses and doing complete cardiovascular system checks, such as EKGs and treadmill tests. During the quarantine, the number of people who have access to the astronauts is restricted. And anyone who does come into contact with them must wear a mask. NASA wants to prevent the astronauts from catching any last-minute infectious diseases or simply a cold. Even the common cold can disrupt a space mission.

Since they are quarantined, it's unlikely that astronauts will get a cold in space. But if they do, it's not fun.

Colds in Space?

The crew of Apollo 7, a 1968 rocket mission from before we landed on the Moon, did catch colds in space. Well, sort of. Doctors think that astronaut Wally Schirra might have been exposed to the common cold before he went up. He may have exposed the other astronauts while in space. Regardless, they all came down with the sniffles and runny noses. You can't blow your nose through a space helmet. The astronauts did what they wanted. They didn't follow the rules. It's a good thing it was a safe landing.

Accidents HAPPEN

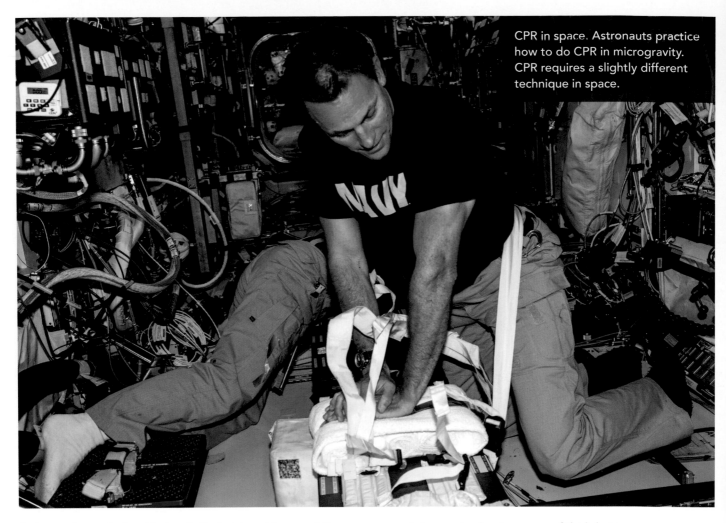

CPR in space. Astronauts practice how to do CPR in microgravity. CPR requires a slightly different technique in space.

Astronauts are trained in basic first aid and have a kit packed with supplies, because you never know when an accident will happen. And yet, while the first aid kit in the ISS might be like the ones on Earth, injuries are treated differently in space.

Let's compare how first aid would be performed on two people—one on Earth, and one in space—with the same injury, a bad cut on one of their legs.

On Earth, a gash, or cut, on the leg bleeds a lot. Blood flows or drips down the leg, depending on how deep the cut is. The first step is to stop that bleeding! Using a gauze pad, someone needs to push down firmly on the cut. This will stop the bleeding. If the cut is not deep, it won't need stitches. Even so, it's best to apply antibiotic ointment and then a bandage. The last step is to wipe up the blood that might have dripped down the person's leg. All done. Easy-peasy.

In space, it's not that easy to get a cut because safety is a big factor on the ISS. But let's assume an astronaut cuts their leg. Will they bleed? Yes. Humans bleed in space just like they do on Earth, but how they bleed is a little different. In microgravity, the blood from a cut doesn't flow downward. Instead, it spurts out in every direction. The blood gushes, spatters, and forms big bubbles and floats around.

Let's say an astronaut is injured. He will call for help. His fellow astronaut quickly responds. She immediately floats to one of the U.S. or Russian modules of the ISS, where the first aid kits are located, and brings the kit back to the injured astronaut. She opens the kit, grabs a gauze pad, and tells him to hang on. (Remember: They are in microgravity.) He grabs on to a handhold to steady himself. The other astronaut pushes the gauze pad hard against his leg. After a few minutes, she carefully pulls the gauze back.

A bubble of blood sits on top of the wound. That's not something you'd see on Earth. But in microgravity, blood forms weird bubbles over a wound. (Scientists aren't exactly sure why.) The wound doesn't look deep, so she carefully squeezes antibiotic ointment onto it and applies a bandage.

The final step is to let the medical team on Earth know what happened. They will want to keep a close eye on the injured astronaut for a few days. They don't want infection to set in. Could that happen? Yep. The air in the ISS, while filtered, isn't exactly the cleanest. It's filled with dead skin cells, particles of food, and even tiny bacteria from an astronaut sneezing (or going to the bathroom). All of these things could possibly get into the open wound and cause infection.

The good thing is, the first aid kit has plenty of drugs to help combat an infection (as well as a few other things, like motion sickness).

TECHNO
TREATMENTS

Perhaps in the future, astronauts will have their very own biocompatible bandages. That's right, these bandages will be made from an astronaut's own cells! These cells will be harvested on the ground, before launching, and suspended in special fluid to keep them alive. If an astronaut happens to get a cut while in space, this cool handheld device could insert their own bioimprinted cells onto the wound, effectively closing it. It's like if you had a bandage made from your own skin. Sounds strange (and maybe even a little gross), but if it works, then you won't have to pack boxes and boxes of bandages if you take that long trip to Mars someday. You could just use your own skin to cover a wound. Pretty cool!

Do cuts take longer to heal in space? —Mila, 11

Yes, they can. Astronauts' immune systems are affected by microgravity. This means cuts may take longer to heal than if they were on Earth. Scientists don't know a lot about this, but they are doing much research on it.

First AID KIT

The Mayo Clinic recommends that everyone (on Earth) keep a well-stocked first aid kit in their homes. It is important to treat wounds right away not only to stop bleeding but also to prevent infection. Kids who are injured or encounter an injured person should tell an adult immediately. If you aren't able to stop the bleeding or if a wound looks serious, contact your doctor or take the injured person to a medical facility immediately.

At a minimum, a first aid kit should include:

- Adhesive tape

- Elastic wrap bandages

- Bandage strips and butterfly bandages in assorted sizes

- Superglue

- Nonstick sterile bandages and roller gauze in assorted sizes

- Instant cold packs

- Cotton balls and cotton-tipped swabs

- Disposable nonlatex examination gloves (several pairs)

- Hand sanitizer

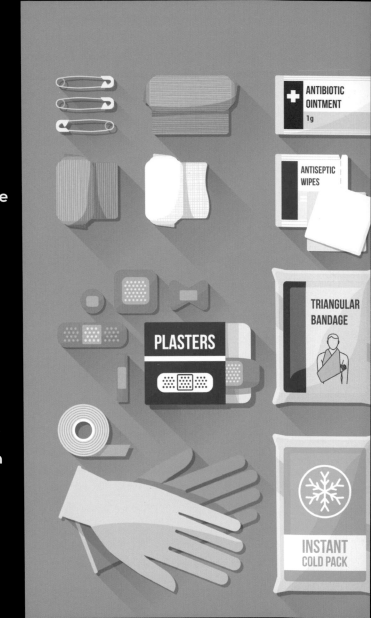

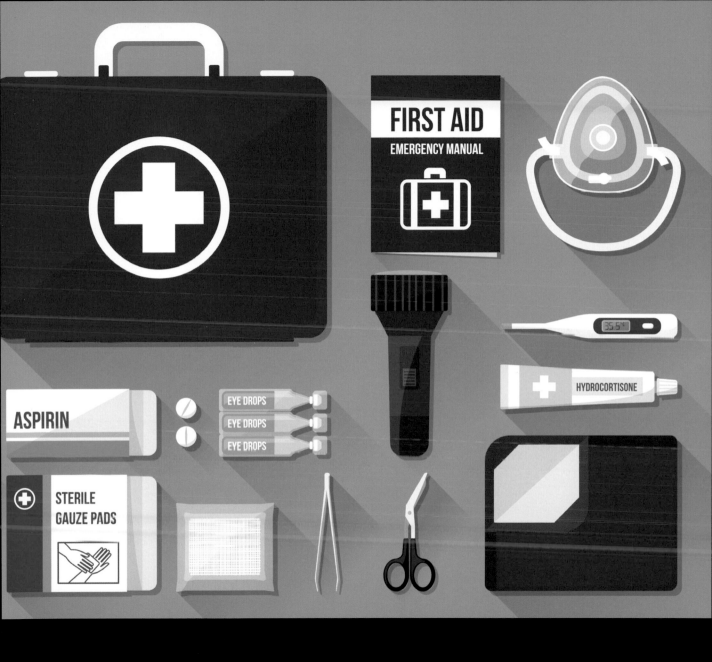

Call the **DOC**

Doctors on the ISS. NASA astronaut (and medical doctor) Andrew Morgan poses with a stethoscope for medical checks inside the laboratory module after an exercise session.

Cuts, bruises, and minor colds are not difficult to deal with on the ISS. The real problem is if an astronaut has a more serious medical issue. After all, there is no emergency room in the ISS. There isn't an ambulance to call in space, either, and the doctors don't make house calls. Well, not in person. A doctor is always only a video call away.

Telemedicine, which became big on Earth during the COVID-19 pandemic, is the way doctors "visit" the ISS. Since the beginning of the space program, doctors have been available to astronauts whenever they need them. This is a good thing. Just having someone who is knowledgeable on the other end of a video call is helpful. However, the doctors cannot perform procedures. That's up to the astronauts themselves.

Sometimes the crew is lucky enough to have an astronaut on board the ISS who is also a medically trained doctor. But that isn't always the case. So astronauts must help each other.

On board the ISS is a modified ultrasound machine. Astronauts are trained to use it to help diagnose problems. They can check their ocular pressure (the pressure in their eye), take a look at the arteries and veins in their necks, and examine their cardiovascular systems (heart and lungs). And they can even check their bone density. All of these things help doctors on the ground diagnose problems.

An injury, especially one that might require surgery, is a serious situation. Presently, it is not possible to conduct surgery in space. Performing surgery would have to be done in an extremely contained area. Otherwise, the blood would leak out of the wound and fly all over the ISS. It would contaminate everything.

Scientists are working on a plan, though. They are testing a device that would cover the wound. Called the aqueous immersion surgical system (AISS), it would form a saline-filled dome over the area. This would keep the person's blood and bodily fluids contained.

An extremely serious infection or injury would require immediate attention, meaning the astronaut would have to be evacuated. While it's not an ambulance, there is always a spacecraft docked to the ISS. In case of emergency, it can make the trip to Earth in about three-and-a-half hours. Thankfully, this has only happened once. A cosmonaut (a Russian astronaut) had to be transported home due to a serious infection.

But as the push to have humans live and work longer in space continues, this is definitely something that needs to be addressed.

> **How quickly can an astronaut get back to Earth if they need to see a doctor? —Sydney, 10**
>
> It depends on where the ISS is in its orbit. While the emergency spacecraft can get a person to Earth in a few hours, it doesn't mean they can get immediate medical attention. It can depend on the spacecraft type too. The Soyuz capsule lands on land. Space X lands in the water. Depending on where the spacecraft lands, the doctors need time to reach the landing site. For this reason, the crew is trained to respond to medical emergencies, and our doctors can talk to us over the radios to help.

Blood CLOTS

Microgravity does strange things to the human body. But no one expected it to cause blood clots. A blood clot, according to the Mayo Clinic, is a "gel-like" clump of blood. This clump occurs when the blood changes from being liquid to partially solid (similar perhaps to the consistency of pudding).

Clots form in the blood because of an injury or a cut. They plug the affected blood vessel—a vein or artery. On Earth, blood clots can happen without an injury to the body, but that is rare. And those instances usually signal that another medical issue is going on.

But in space, blood clots can happen to healthy people. Another surprising condition was that blood could reverse its flow in the body.

How was this discovered? A group of doctors on Earth proposed a research project in space. They wondered how the blood flow in the jugular veins was affected by microgravity. The jugular veins run down either side of the windpipe. You can try to feel them by putting your fingers on your neck and applying slight pressure. Feel that thumping? That's blood pumping through your veins. While arteries pump blood to the brain, once the oxygen is removed, the veins pump the blood back to the heart.

For the research project, eleven astronauts were asked to take ultrasounds of their necks. These astronauts had been on board for six months. One astronaut would use the ultrasound to take a reading on another astronaut's neck.

Ultrasounds do not hurt. They send sound waves through the body to get a picture of what's inside. The neck ultrasounds allowed doctors to see blood flowing through the jugular vein.

What they saw was unexpected. Of the eleven astronauts, six of them had stagnant or reverse blood flow. That means that either their blood was flowing much slower than normal, or it was flowing in reverse. Instead of moving down from the head, the blood appeared to be moving up into the head. And the biggest shock was that one astronaut actually had a blood clot in her jugular vein. And another astronaut had a partial blood clot.

Helping out: Astronaut Jessica Meir takes an ultasound of Astronaut Andrew Morgan's veins for a research project

A blood clot in a jugular vein is very serious. It could break off and flow into the heart, which would cause a heart attack. Or it could go to the brain and cause a stroke. Both conditions are life-threatening—not something anyone wants to deal with in space.

It's a good thing that the blood clots were found. Doctors immediately conferred with the astronauts who had the clots. They were put on a special drug called an anticoagulant. This is medicine that helps to dissolve the clot and keep more from forming. Both astronauts were carefully watched. Eventually, the clots dissolved, and everyone was fine.

What about the reverse blood flow? Scientists aren't exactly sure why that happens. But it didn't appear to affect the astronauts at all. When the astronauts came back to Earth, everything went back to normal. Researchers are still studying this phenomenon.

While they don't have all the answers, doctors learned a lot from this research program. They now know that it is important to carefully track blood flow in humans who are in space for long periods of time. All of this information is used to develop future technology that might help prevent blood clots from happening again. After all, an astronaut working or living on the Moon would be even farther—possibly as much as three days or more—away from the nearest emergency room!

TECHNO

TREATMENTS

Meet the Russian Chibis Suit. These rubber suction pants are on board the ISS to help astronauts apply lower body negative pressure (LBNP). When astronauts spend a long time in space, fluids can start to shift to the upper body. When this happens, they climb inside the pants. Once they are on, a button is flipped and the air in the pants is sucked out. This pressure effectively counteracts microgravity and pulls fluids and blood back to the legs. It's like having a vacuum cleaner attached to your pants. It might sound weird, but it works! Astronauts are experimenting taking time in the Chibis Suit to offset the long-term effects of microgravity.

Mayo Medi-Facts

Blood clots require prompt attention. If someone believes they have a blood clot, they should contact their doctor immediately. Signs to look for are swelling under the skin, redness, or pain in an arm or leg. A possible blood clot in the lung could cause difficulty breathing. Get to an emergency room immediately!

Keeping CLEAN

Chores on the ISS. Astronaut Kayla Barron cleans water lines on the ISS to prevent particles from building up.

Unfortunately, going to space does not get an astronaut out of weekly chores. That's right. They do chores on the ISS! Once a week, each area of the ISS is scrubbed clean. This is not just so the astronauts have something to do. Cleaning keeps everything sanitized. Germs can still grow in a sealed, enclosed space such as the ISS.

Since everyone up there needs to stay healthy, the only way to do that is to keep the ISS spotless. Well, as close to spotless as possible.

The main difference between chores on Earth and chores in space is that when you clean a kitchen at home, most of the mess stays on the countertops, the table, or the floor. However, on the ISS, the galley, or kitchen, could have spaghetti sauce on the walls … or ceiling. Remember, liquids float everywhere. And wherever they land, they stay.

Each crew sets up their own schedule. But basically, people clean the galley, airlock, bathroom, gym, and laboratories.

Astronauts scrub walls, floors, and ceilings. They pay particular attention to anything that might be stuck in small corners and spaces. You never know where that pizza sauce or ketchup will travel. They don't use wet paper towels or sponges. They only use disinfectant wipes.

Yes, that means that it's someone's job to clean the bathroom, too. (Although everyone is supposed to clean the bathroom after they use it. But sometimes that isn't enough.) Cleanup usually takes place Saturday morning and can be a whole crew affair.

Each astronaut is responsible for keeping their own crew cabin clean. Four astronauts sleep in Node 2. Two astronauts sleep in the Russian segment. The ISS has had as many as thirteen people on board at once. Those without crew cabins slept in their spacecraft capsule. Or they strung up hammocks and slept in one of the nodes. The crew cabin is not that big. But during the astronauts' time on the ISS, it is all theirs. They usually clean it with disinfectant wipes as needed. Cleanliness is important for every area on the ISS.

The air cleaners on the ISS do a fantastic job of sucking dirt, hair, and particles out of the air. However, the cleaners have filters, and hair can clog the filters and prevent them from working properly. That's why the filters have to be vacuumed at least once a week— the vents, too.

Most astronauts agree that cleaning in the ISS is the same as cleaning at home. If people develop good cleaning habits and clean regularly, then the ISS stays shipshape for all.

Living with Microbe Friends

Scientists estimate that fifty-five different kinds of microorganisms live with the astronauts on the ISS. How did they get there? They were brought up by humans. Or on the supplies. These bacteria, molds, fungi, viruses, and protozoa have adapted well to space life. They don't bother the humans, and the humans don't bother them. But some of these tiny creatures, called technophiles, love to munch on metal. It's up to the astronauts to clean off the equipment regularly to prevent that.

MAYO MEDI-FACTS

Microbes, or germs, are everywhere! They live in the air, on the ground, in food, and in water. People can't escape them. For the most part, that's fine. A human's immune system keeps them safe. Microbes help humans to stay healthy by aiding in digestion and other things. But once in a while, microbes can make people sick. That's when they should see a doctor.

CHAPTER FOUR

LABS IN SPACE

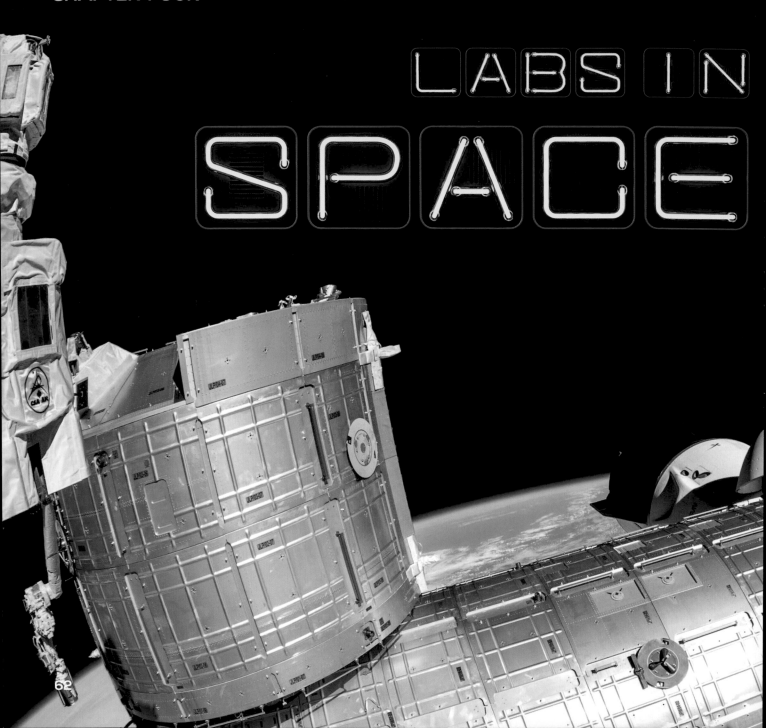

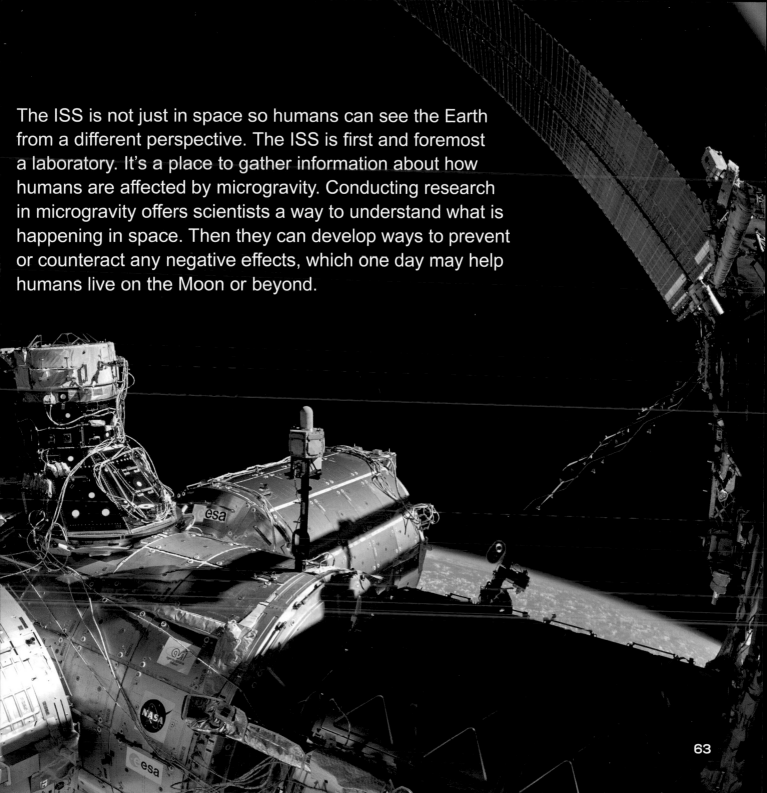

The ISS is not just in space so humans can see the Earth from a different perspective. The ISS is first and foremost a laboratory. It's a place to gather information about how humans are affected by microgravity. Conducting research in microgravity offers scientists a way to understand what is happening in space. Then they can develop ways to prevent or counteract any negative effects, which one day may help humans live on the Moon or beyond.

Muscles to MOVE

Technology to help keep fit. NASA astronaut Victor Glover installs research gear that will study the effects of spaceflight on musculoskeletal disease.

It is a well-known fact that humans living in space lose muscle mass. That means their muscles get smaller. As mentioned before, without gravity, there is no resistance to keep the muscles strong. But scientists wanted to know more. What is actually causing this loss of muscle mass on a cellular level? Is something happening to the cells in the muscles themselves that is causing them to get smaller?

For that answer, one research project turned to worms. The roundworm *Caenorhabditis elegans*, in fact. It sounds weird, but this particular roundworm is similar to humans. Its muscle structure and metabolism (how the muscle processes energy) at the cellular level is a lot like human muscles. So much so, that these worms show the

same muscle issues in microgravity as humans. When scientists realized this, they were thrilled.

The *C. elegans* is very small, only about one millimeter in length. It does not have a heart or a circulatory system, and it only lives for three days. It has 959 cells, and it reproduces quickly. All of these characteristics make this roundworm great for research!

So, how does this work? Do the astronauts do the research on the ISS? Not exactly. The *C. elegans* roundworms were sent to the ISS. These worms "lived" in space for six months. Don't worry, they were kept in their own special sample containers.

During the first experiment, scientists were looking at the muscle fibers of the worm—the very parts (fibers) that make up the muscle. Astronauts left one group of worms live in microgravity. They took another group and placed them into a centrifuge machine. The worms were spun around so that they felt the force of 1 g on them. At the end of the project, the worms were sent back to Earth and studied.

What did the scientists discover? The worms appeared to adapt to space the same way humans do. They changed what they eat and how they moved. The next step was to understand why this happened.

The scientists sent up a second batch of worms. This time they learned that the roundworms have special protein complexes in their muscles. These complexes help to build more muscle. But they can also make the muscle smaller. When the worms were in microgravity, the protein complexes reduced the size of the muscles. This could be similar to what happens in the human body.

Scientists plan to continue studying the *C. elegans* roundworm. They hope that one day they'll understand why muscles lose so much mass in space. And the information from this research doesn't just help people in microgravity. It could be used to help people on Earth, including those who have osteoporosis (brittle bones) or whose muscles break down because of extended bed rest. Who knew a microscopic worm could help with all of that?

Mayo Medi-Facts

Osteoporosis is a disease that causes bones to become brittle. It occurs because bone tissue is not being created as fast as it is breaking down. While osteoporosis occurs more often to older people, it can happen to anyone.

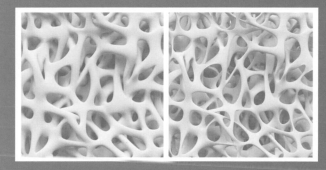

normal   osteoporosis

Meet the *C. elegans* roundworm

This tiny creature is an invertebrate. That means it doesn't have a backbone like humans do. Its skin is also transparent, so its insides are visible. It has a mouth at one end and releases its waste at the other. There may be as many as 50,000 species of roundworms on Earth. In space, as far as anyone knows, there is one.

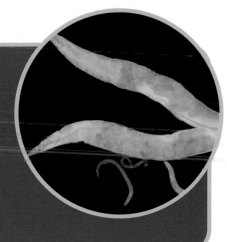

What's on THE MENU?

Tending to the plants. NASA astronauts Jessica Watkins and Bob Hines work on the XROOTS space botany investigation to understand how plants grow in space.

Time to eat! For some people on Earth that means sitting down to a table and eating their fill of fresh fruits and vegetables. That's not exactly how astronauts eat. But it soon may be. Well, not the sitting at the table part, unless they are hooked into the chairs. Still, the fresh fruits and vegetables part is happening now. And the food is being grown on the ISS itself. That's right. It's a garden in space!

Doctors have long known the benefits of eating fresh food. Back around the 17th century, sailors would go months without fresh fruits and vegetables when they were out at sea. This caused them to develop scurvy, a nasty disease that was due to a lack of vitamin C. It caused wounds on the shins, painful joints, and even bleeding gums. Ouch! The good thing was that the cure was simple—eat more fruits and veggies. When sailors changed their diets, they were cured.

Space exploration is a lot like seafaring: People are gone for long periods of time. The ISS receives regular supplies of fresh fruits and vegetables. But how will that work when humans are on the Moon (over three to four days away) or on Mars (about nine months away!)? How awesome would it be if astronauts could grow their own food on the Moon? Or on Mars? And more important, could it be done?

That's what scientists want to find out. What started as a research project has turned into a full-blown garden in space. The first greenhouse sent up to space in 2002 was called the Lada. It was mounted on the wall in the Russian module. At first, scientists just wanted to see if roots would grow in microgravity. They were thrilled to find out they could.

Eventually, a slightly larger space garden called Veggie, the Vegetable Production System, was added in 2014. This greenhouse is about the size of a piece of carry-on luggage. It has growing compartments for each of the different foods. The "soil" is not dirt from Earth. Instead, seeds are placed into plant "pillows." The pillows contain a special clay that acts as the soil. The pillows also have fertilizer and water. Those two things are released over time to keep the plants fed and watered. The astronauts don't have to do much to tend the garden, unlike on Earth. No weeds grow up there! All they have to do is ensure the 70-watt LED lights stay on. The lights have a magenta glow because that is the wavelength of light the plants like best.

Meals on the ISS now include fresh lettuce (three kinds), radishes, mizuna mustard greens, red Russian kale, bok choi, and zinnia (flowers). Next up? Experimenting with growing berries, beans, tomatoes, and peppers. All the things needed for a great salad!

TECHNO

TREATMENTS

Growing food in space isn't easy. The plant must get enough water, but not too much. Enough fertilizer, but not too much. But one of the biggest challenges is that a bubble of humidity and oxygen can form over the plants. Remember that liquids form bubbles in space. Humid air is just air with water in it. If a bubble forms over a plant, it will keep the plant in hot, moist conditions. Not all plants need that. So, Veggie is placed near a fan, which keeps air flowing around the plants. And it also prevents the bubble from forming.

Why would they grow flowers in space? —Annabelle, 9

Scientists wanted to know if something could grow in space over a long period of time. They sent up zinnia seeds. The seeds stayed in space for over a year and a half. They grew into beautiful flowers. This is proof that it might be possible to grow plants such as tomatoes—which will be much tastier than a flower. Our crew grew the most complicated crop to date during our mission—Hatch chiles! I got to hand pollinate the flowers myself! We also got to eat them, and they were very tasty! Fresh food can provide much needed vitamins and minerals, as well as benefits to mental health.

Space GARDEN

NASA has created its very own greenhouse (of sorts) on Earth where it grows all different types of plants. Although this is for research, it's also for dinner! Astronauts can munch on radish, cucumbers, cabbage, kale, and much more. Scientists are learning how fruits and vegetables grow in space. After all, the nearest grocery store is thousands of miles away.

The research conducted by astronauts on board the ISS helps NASA understand how to grow plants on the Moon one day. One experiment has even successfully grown plants in regolith, the rocky lunar soil! Farms in space? It could happen.

Some of these plants may eventually be grown in space. But for now, astronauts on the ISS can munch on radishes, cucumbers, cabbage, kale, and much more.

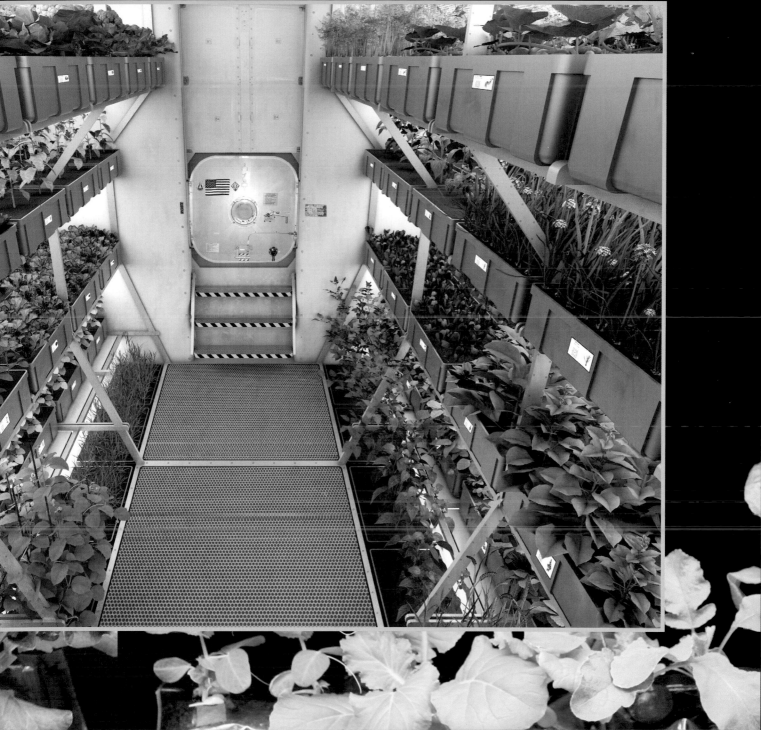

Squid IN SPACE

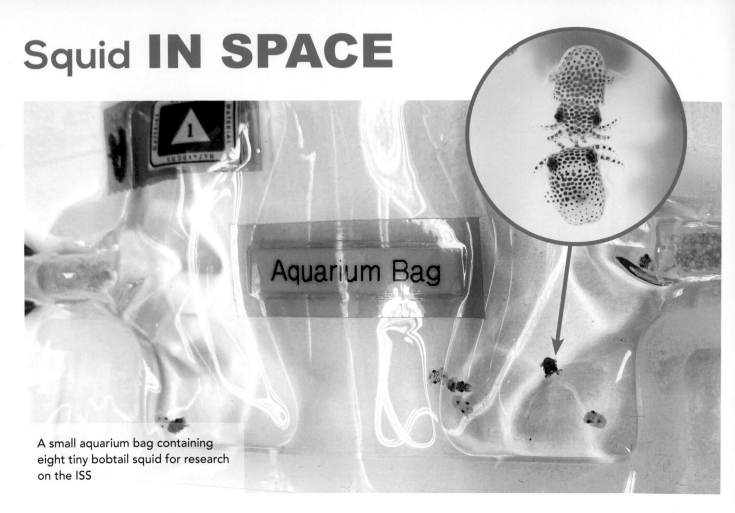

A small aquarium bag containing eight tiny bobtail squid for research on the ISS

While it might sound like a great title for a sci-fi movie, scientists did actually send squid to space. Not the big ones you see in the ocean. Especially not the giant squid. Scientists sent baby Hawaiian bobtail squid. These colorful creatures are usually only about one-tenth of an inch long. Like all squid, they have two big eyes and eight legs. These cephalopods also light up, just like fireflies. They use bioluminescence, a light produced by a chemical reaction inside their bodies.

The cool thing about these squid is that they have bacteria inside them. The bacteria help to control the amount of light they give off. When the squid swims at night, it is lit up. That means predators can see it easily. The bacteria or microbes living inside of the squid dim that light. The microbes match the color of their light, so the squid look invisible.

Why would this be a cool thing to study? Scientists believed that the relationship between the microbes and the squid might change in space. They were right! Microgravity does affect the microbes. While the research isn't complete, these squid may give clues to how the human immune system is affected by space.

The immune system is a human's basic defense mechanism. It's a network of white blood cells, organs, antibodies (proteins), and chemicals that fight off disease and infection. A strong immune system keeps people healthy.

Scientists know that astronaut's immune systems don't always work normally in microgravity. Sometimes the system doesn't recognize bacteria as a threat. Scientists aren't sure why this happens. But the body doesn't activate to prevent the bacteria from growing and spreading. That causes infection. The last thing astronauts want is to be sick in space. A bacterial infection can get serious very quickly if it isn't treated. While there are antibiotics on the ISS, it's better if the immune system can fight the bacteria itself.

That's where the squid come in. Understanding how the bacterial microbes change their relationship with squid can help. It might give scientists a clue as to how the human immune system changes in microgravity. Then they could figure out a way to prevent this from happening. Or at least boost the immune system into fighting the bacteria itself.

Who knew squid in space could be so helpful and important?

Mayo Medi-Facts

You can keep your immune system healthy by washing your hands. Eating healthy foods and getting exercise also. If you feel sick, call your doctor. They will know if it is a serious infection that needs to be treated. Sometimes sickness can be fought off by the immune system. All it needs is time and rest.

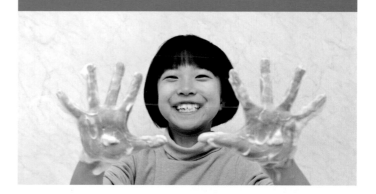

Camouflage Squid

Hawaiian squid are found in the ocean around the Hawaiian Islands. Every morning they expel, or push out, most of the bacteria living inside them. Then the squid bury themselves in the sand. While they are "resting" in the sand, new bacteria enter their bodies. So, at night, when the squid are up, they glow again. But they have new bacteria to dim their inner bioluminescence (light). The U.S. Air Force has studied these squid for years to develop a material like the bacteria that would camouflage their planes.

Helping All **HEARTS**

A cell containing engineered heart tissues to help scientists understand what happens to heart muscles in space

Microgravity offers a way for scientists to perform experiments they might not be able to do on Earth. One example is studying heart disease. The research being conducted on the ISS is not for astronauts necessarily. After all, they are extremely healthy people. But the findings of this study may help people on Earth. The goal is to understand how a condition called ischemic cardiomyopathy works at the cellular level.

Heart disease is a huge problem. It affects one in every four adults. And it is responsible for more than 600,000 deaths a year in the United States. Ischemic cardiomyopathy is the weakening of the heart muscle. This can be due to a heart attack or heart disease.

Where does space come in? It is a well-known fact that the heart muscles of astronauts change in microgravity. The heart doesn't have to pump as hard because there is very little gravity. It normally takes a lot of pumping to get blood and fluids up from the legs. But in space, not so much. So, like any muscle that isn't used as frequently, the heart muscles start to weaken. The longer an astronaut is in space, the weaker the heart becomes.

This makes space the perfect place to study ischemic cardiomyopathy. Since this condition occurs naturally, it's easier to study. Of course, the study is not being conducted on the astronauts themselves. Instead, researchers sent up hundreds of heart tissue cells.

Cryopreservation

The heart cells are transferred to the ISS through a process called cryopreservation. They are frozen to approximately minus 112°F (-80°C). That is cold! This is done in a controlled manner so as not to damage the cells. Then when the cells get up to the ISS, they are transferred to a special enclosed area. The astronaut works on the cells by using gloves inside an area closed off by a plastic bubble or box. The research must be conducted quickly once the cells arrive. Otherwise they get too warm and the project won't work.

These are special cells, called human induced pluripotent stem cells (iPSCs). The original cells come from the blood or skin of humans on Earth. They are then transported to space and put into the lab. In the lab, the iPSCs are grown in a petri dish.

Astronaut Kate Rubins, a microbiologist, worked with the iPSCs during her time on the ISS. She did the work on the initial project in 2016. The data gathered was very promising. So much so, that a second project was sent up in 2021. This time the cells were 3-D heart tissue samples. The research team wanted to understand if engineered heart tissue would react the same way in microgravity.

The information gathered from these experiments is still being evaluated, but it could one day help doctors find more ways to aid heart patients, such as helping people who've suffered heart attacks live longer. Or it might even help prevent heart attacks. The astronauts on the ISS don't just study how people live in space. They are also learning more about the human body to help people on Earth.

Mayo Medi-Facts

Heart disease is a serious condition. It can cause irregular heartbeats, pain or tightness in the chest, numbness in the arms or legs, or even pain in the jaw, neck, or belly. These are all signals that a person should visit their doctor. While there are other conditions that could cause these symptoms, it's a good idea to get them checked out. Treatment can definitely help someone with heart issues.

The TWIN STUDY

Twins! Commander and astronaut Scott Kelly right along with his brother, astronaut Mark Kelly. Scott Kelly spent a 1-year mission aboard the International Space Station.

One of the most unique research programs NASA has undertaken was studying twins. Mark Kelly and Scott Kelly are identical twins. They are both astronauts. Identical twins have the same genetics. Genes are made of DNA, the code that tells our cells how to act. Identical twins don't have identical DNA, but it's very close.

Close enough for scientists to wonder, what would happen if one twin lived for 340 days on the ISS, while the other lived on Earth? Would the twin in space exhibit different traits? Would his eyesight change? Would

his DNA be affected? These questions are important. The answers might help us understand how humans are affected by living in space. How would the different environments affect each twin?

During the experiment, Scott Kelly went to space. Before he left, he and Mark both had complete medical work-ups. Doctors recorded a baseline, or general idea, of what was going on in their bodies. Then, in March 2015, Scott blasted off. He lived on the ISS for 340 days. At the time, it was one of the longest stretches an

American had been in space. During the time Scott was in space, both brothers participated in periodic medical checkups. They gave blood, had their blood pressure taken, and participated in many other tests.

Most of the changes to Scott's body went back to normal within six months of being back on Earth. A few changes to his DNA, however, did not return to normal. Is that a bad thing? Scientists don't think so.

What did this study discover? It appears that long-term spaceflight does not have a significant effect on the human body. It is subjective, however, meaning that every person is different. Some people do have issues that come up during spaceflight that others do not. But overall, living in space appears to be relatively safe for humans.

Scientists at NASA's Human Research Program continue to study all astronauts that go to space. The more they can learn about the human body in microgravity, the better. They are using all of this data to create preventive measures to keep problems from developing. And to create ways to deal with issues that might occur in space.

All of this work may one day help humans to live and work for long periods of time on the Moon or Mars.

AT THE END OF THE MISSION

After Scott came home, both brothers went through even more tests. Scientists compared the findings for both twins and came up with some interesting results:

- Scott's eyes changed structurally due to the extra fluid in his head.

- Scott's cognitive function, how he thinks, remained the same, but he was a bit slower and less accurate when he first returned to Earth. (That eventually returned to normal.)

- Scott's gene expression, which tells cells how to respond in an environment, was changed.

Mayo Medi-Facts

Identical twins are formed when a single fertilized egg splits into two different eggs. Identical twins are always the same gender. Their genes are so similar that if one twin needs glasses to improve their vision, it's likely that the other will, too. The chance of having identical twins is about three in one thousand births. So, on the whole, not very likely.

What is next for space medicine? There is so much to explore.

As humans continue to live and work in space, NASA will be there to keep them healthy. Space medicine will continue to expand to one day address the needs of living on the Moon. Perhaps it will solve the problem of how to handle emergencies without having to send people back to Earth. And maybe even develop a way to perform surgery in microgravity. It may even develop innovative technologies using virtual reality to help support mental health issues that may be encountered on long, lonely voyages through space. And the amazing technologies created for astronauts will also help humans on Earth—even those who will never go to space.

GLOSSARY

Atmospheric pressure—the pressure exerted on an object or living organism by the weight of the atmosphere

Atrophy—when a body part begins to waste away, possibly because it's not being used

Behavioral health—the study of emotions, behaviors, and biology relating to a person's mental health

Blood volume—the amount of blood circulating in the body

Bone density—the measurement of how much minerals are in your bones

Circadian rhythm—the 24-hour cycle of a person's internal "clock"

Cupola—the domed windows where astronauts can view space and the Earth

Dieticians—an expert on diet and nutrition

DNA—the genetic material that determines how an organism looks and functions

Dosimeter—a device used to measure the amount of ionizing radiation a person experiences

Drought-tolerant—plants that are able to survive with little access to water

EKG—an electrocardiogram, or a device that measures the electrical activity of the heart

Flight surgeon—a person in the military who is a doctor specializing in aerospace medicine

Free fall—an object that is falling while only experiencing gravity

Gene expression—the process where the information in a gene is turned into a protein

Immune system—a part of the body that prevents or manages infections

Microgravity—an environment with little gravity where objects appear weightless

Optic nerve—the part of the body that transmits signals from the eye to the brain

Orbit—the curved motion around another object

Radiation—energy, like electromagnetic energy, that travels very fast as a particle or a wave

Rotorcraft—a rotary-wing aircraft, like a helicopter

Trifocals—glasses that have three different prescriptions within one lens

Ultrasound—a medical test that uses sound waves to capture a picture of the inside of an organism

INDEX

Learn More

Books to Read

Astronaut-Aquanaut: How Space Science and Sea Science Interact by Jennifer Swanson (National Geographic Kids, 2015)

Astronaut Handbook by Meghan McCarthy (Dragonfly Books, 2017)

Gutsy Girls Go For Science: Astronauts: With Stem Projects for Kids by Alicia Klepeis (Nomad Press, 2019)

Other Resources

NASA at Home—activities, information, and tons of fun facts and photos. *https://www.nasa.gov/nasa-at-home-for-kids-and-families*

Solve It! for Kids podcast—hear from real astronauts, NASA engineers, and more about how they build rockets, spacecrafts, and live in space. https://solveitforkids.com/

Illustrations Credits